How to be an effective teacher in higher education

How to be an effective teacher in higher education

Answers to lecturers' questions

Alan Mortiboys

Open University Press

Open University Press
McGraw-Hill Education
McGraw-Hill House
Shoppenhangers Road
Maidenhead
Berkshire
England
SL6 2QL

email: enquiries@openup.co.uk
world wide web: www.openup.co.uk

and Two Penn Plaza, New York, NY 10121–2289, USA

First published 2010

Copyright © Mortiboys 2010

A catalogue record of this book is available from the British Library

ISBN-13: 978-0-33-523740-1 (pb) 978-0-33-523739-5 (hb)
ISBN-10: 0335237401 (pb) 0335237398 (hb)

Library of Congress Cataloging-in-Publication Data
CIP data applied for

Typeset by RefineCatch Limited, Bungay, Suffolk
Printed in the UK by Bell & Bain Ltd, Glasgow

Fictitious names of companies, products, people, characters and/or data that
may be used herein (in case studies or in examples) are not intended to represent
any real individual, company, product or event.

Mixed Sources
Product group from well-managed
forests and other controlled sources
www.fsc.org   Cert no. TT-COC-002769
© 1996 Forest Stewardship Council

The **McGraw·Hill** Companies

For Mary

Contents

Acknowledgements

I must first of all thank the hundreds of lecturers who have supplied the questions that led to the idea and the framework for this book.

Thanks also to Sian Howarth and Matt Smith of Birmingham City University for their contributions.

Thanks to my wife Mary for her support and extreme patience.

I especially want to thank Bob Farmer and not just for some of his material that I have adapted for the book. Thanks, Bob, for your illuminating insights into learning and teaching in higher education, for being such an inspiration both as a teacher and as a learner, and for your unfailing good humour and sense of fun.

Introduction

This book sets out to provide practical answers to the most commonly recurring questions that lecturers ask about teaching groups in higher education.

I have run scores of workshops and short courses in recent years for university lecturers, on aspects of learning, teaching, and assessment. Both new and experienced lecturers have attended these workshops, many of which focus on teaching in the classroom or lecture theatre, with titles such as 'Developing Student Motivation through Active Learning' and 'Large Group Teaching'.

I often provide the opportunity, at a midpoint in the workshop, for participants to think of 'the one question I would like an answer to before the end of the course' and to write it on a piece of paper. I collect these and then create time later for me and other participants to respond to the questions where they have not been directly covered by the programme. This section of the programme attracts particular interest and engagement by participants. I have always kept these questions after the event and, when preparing to run it again, consulted them to remind me of the perspective of participants and of their concerns when teaching groups.

Eventually, I came to realize that the questions I had collected, which ran into the hundreds, encompassed all of the information and guidance sought by lecturers (mostly new lecturers) about teaching groups in higher education. That was the origin of the idea for this book and the questions have shaped its structure and content.

I have selected fifty-five questions* to answer. All of them are verbatim as asked by an individual, anonymously. Often, the question I have chosen is representative of many more on the same theme.

I have attempted to answer the questions in the spirit in which they were asked – that is, looking for a brief, practical response. However, I have

* If there is a question that you would like to see included should there be a second edition of this book, please contact me at: alan.mortiboys@btinternet.com.

taken the opportunity on occasion to go beyond the intended focus of the question to consider, for instance, the influence of external factors on what happens in the classroom or to explore differing interpretations of what it means to be a teacher. I have also included references to relevant literature in the hope of tempting the reader to explore further. In addition, there are fourteen tasks interspersed through the book that are intended to help the reader apply the answer to their own practice in teaching. These tasks might also be used as triggers for exercises or discussion on courses on learning and teaching in higher education.

I have grouped the questions and the answers to them into ten 'chapters,' but each chapter simply contains a cluster of questions on a similar theme, or, in two instances, just a single question. The book is not intended to be read sequentially and I hope that readers will simply start with the questions that grab their attention.

The book does not attempt to address all of the various activities related to teaching that the higher education lecturer engages in. It is not about creating and making assessments, devising online learning, personal tutoring, and so on. It is not about the scholarship of teaching and it does not present a critique of theories of learning and teaching in higher education. It focuses on what for so many new lecturers is their most pressing concern – what to do when they find themselves for a designated period of time in a room with a group of learners who they are responsible for teaching. Incidentally, I have used the term 'session' to describe that occasion, which the individual lecturer might refer to as a lecture, class, seminar, tutorial, lab session or workshop.

1 Planning and preparation

Question 1: Having never done any teaching or lecturing, what is the best way to approach a first session?

When preparing for any session with a group of learners, a very useful first question to ask is, 'What do I want the learners to have achieved by the end of the session?' This is not the question that many lecturers, even very experienced ones, usually ask. They are more likely to think, 'What do I know and how can I get it across?' or 'Which slides shall I use and in what order?' However, for more effective teaching and learning it is more helpful to consider where you want the learners to get to by the end of the session. This applies whether you describe your session as a lecture, a seminar, a tutorial, a lab session or a workshop.

I will use the term 'objectives' to describe what it is you want the learners to achieve. It may well be that in your institution the term 'outcomes' or 'learning outcomes' is prescribed. In a sense, what term you use does not matter, as long as you begin with the question, 'What do I want the learners to achieve?'

Objectives are usually worded as follows:

'By the end of this session, you will be able to:

- List five local community organizations responsible for health maintenance, or
- Explain the evolution of the landscape of the study area from its pre-industrialized condition to its post-industrialized arrangement, or
- Compare Hofstede's theory of intercultural encounters with Trompenaar's theory of cross-cultural management.'

Task 1
Take a session you have run recently or will be running soon and word an objective for that session. To determine whether your objective is useful, scrutinize it by asking the following three questions.

Will it be clear to your audience?

This implies that you will state or display or distribute these objectives at the start of the session. For many learners, this can enhance their learning. Although all group members will know that the topic is 'stakeholder analysis in project management', they will not know what aspect of 'stakeholder analysis in project management' you want them to be able to explain, analyse, use, and so on. Knowing the objectives will assist many learners in focusing their efforts and attention during the session. It can also help if you refer back to the objectives from time to time during the session, to signpost what has been dealt with and what remains.

The other point behind this question is to ensure that you do not stray into using ambiguous terms or jargon in wording objectives. If you say that 'by the end of the session, you will be able to critically reflect on ...', be ready for learners to take differing conceptions of exactly what that means. Alternatively, an objective such as 'identify the key issues concerned with market analysis in a brewing case study' is unlikely to be open to misinterpretation.

Is it assessable?

You and/or your learners may want to establish the extent to which the objectives have been achieved at the end of the session. This does not necessarily mean a formal assessment. It may take the form of you asking a few questions for learners to answer individually or in pairs, or it may be that each learner says to him or herself, 'Well have I achieved that?' It is important that some conclusion can be reached about whether the objectives have been met. To assist this, make sure that the verb that begins each objective is an 'action verb' – that is, one that lends itself to being assessed, however sketchily. For instance:

> 'Apply basic statistical and numerical skills to the problem of stress in a listed building'.

Two verbs that lecturers often use in objectives that are notoriously difficult to assess are the 'U' word and the 'A' word – 'understand' and 'appreciate'. They are fine words and it is natural to use them to describe desired achievements but they are just about impossible to assess. By the end of the session, the learner may indeed have 'an understanding of Derrida's theory of poststructuralism', but whether it is the correct understanding or indeed of any use at all is another matter.

Is it realistic?

It is easy to forget the starting point and perspective of your learners in relation to the topic of the session. You are running the session because you are expert in the topic. You know a great deal about it. You are also probably very enthusiastic about it because you love the topic or at least enjoy investigating it/ doing it/talking about it. Expertise and enthusiasm are splendid things but can be dangerous for your learners because they can lead you to set objectives that are unrealistic given the existing knowledge of your learners, the number in the class, the time available, and the learners' motivation or lack of it. So, ask yourself, 'Are those objectives achievable in this context? Do I need to pare them down?'

Use these three questions – 'Will it be clear to your audience?', 'Is it assessable?', and 'Is it realistic?' – to check that you have a useful objective or set of objectives for the session. Once you have articulated these objectives, they can be the basis for the rest of your planning. They can guide you in determining what you should say and do during the session, what you want your learners to do during the session, what materials to use, and when and how to use them.

A common criticism of this approach is that it can constrain rather than guide learning. At its worst, focusing on objectives does not recognize that unplanned, incidental learning can happen and such learning may even be discouraged if you are too prescriptive about objectives. Sometimes it is appropriate to word objectives less prescriptively and encourage diversity in learning. For example:

'By the end of the session you will have:

- created your own …
- defined your personal stance on …
- determined what is of most interest to you in relation to …'

Articulating clear objectives can have a vital role in planning and delivering an effective teaching session but it is important not to allow them to shrink the learning possibilities of your group. Questions 3 and 18 provide further guidance on how to plan and prepare for a session after you have decided on the objectives.

There are other things that you may want to happen in a session, which are not directly related to the learners' achievement of specific objectives. This is particularly true of a first session in a module or with any group that you will be meeting on a regular basis.

Task 2

Imagine you are meeting a new group for the first time. List what needs to be done and said by you and by the learners in that session, outside of activities directly related to the session objectives.

It is likely that each item on your list will fall into one of two categories: exchange of information or setting the climate. *Exchange of information* can include:

- telling your learners details about yourself, the module content, the assessment, how you can be contacted, your role, and their role in the sessions;
- the learners telling you their names, existing knowledge, expectations, fears, assumptions, hopes, and so on.

The second category of *setting the climate* is less tangible. It can include:

- providing an opportunity for each person to introduce themselves or one other to the rest of the group;
- ensuring that they are sufficiently enthused to want to come back next week.

Some examples of how to do this can be found in the answer to Question 9.

You will have to decide how much emphasis and time should be given to each of the above. (This may well be determined by the size of the group since hearing from learners becomes less practical as the numbers increase.) A useful question to ask to help you in doing this is, 'How do I want the learners to feel about the module when they leave at the end of the session?' I guess you will want them to feel informed, prepared, and motivated. Too much time spent by you conveying dry information could leave them feeling overwhelmed, bored, and uninterested. Too much time spent attending to the climate at the expense of clear information could leave them feeling frustrated, ill-prepared, and unmotivated.

Question 2: Should there be an optimum number of objectives for any one session?

When you set about writing objectives for a session and find you have a list of, say, ten in total, ask yourself the following three questions:

1. Are you being realistic? As noted above, given the starting point of the learners, given the numbers in the group, given the time available, are those objectives achievable?
2. Could some of those objectives be subsumed under a single objective?
3. Will the learners benefit from seeing this list at the beginning of the session? Normally two, three or even four crisply and clearly worded

objectives should be enough to make clear what the session is about without drowning the learners in detail from the start.

Whatever the length of the session, if you have any more than five objectives you should ask these questions.

Question 3: When preparing to give a lecture, how do you decide what to talk about/what to include?

Based on the assumption that you are familiar with the topic area (which is not always the case – see Question 48), your task is to determine which parts to include and from those which to emphasize. The best starting point is to refer to your objectives (see Question 1).

It is then worth asking yourself what priorities you have for the group; these may already have informed the objectives.

- Do you want them primarily to get an overview or framework?
- Is your main concern that they are motivated and interested enough to follow up the session by finding out more?
- Is it the kind of topic for which it is more productive for the learners to end the session with more questions than answers?
- Or do you simply want them to be exposed to as much information as possible?
  (Note that spending all of your time with the group just providing information is generally not productive – see Question 5.)

It is also important for you to check on the context when determining content. Again, this may already have informed the objectives. Setting the lecture in context includes how it relates to:

- the aims and the learning outcomes of the module;
- previous and future sessions;
- the assessment.

If you are not the module leader and in particular if you are a visiting lecturer, it is important that you establish this context, initially for yourself. Being able to see the bigger picture and to see where this lecture fits into it is a great aid to learning. John Biggs (2003: 75) identifies a 'well-structured knowledge base' as a key component in encouraging a deep approach to learning (see Question 11). If the teacher does not have it, the learners will find it harder to grasp. Once you have a firm grasp of the context, plan for when and how you are going to convey this to the learners. Most of this will be in your introduction but look for opportunities during the session to reinforce how content relates to the rest of the module and to the assessment.

Having considered the objectives, your priorities, and the context, many teachers then find it useful to sift through the possible content and prioritize in the following way:

- Determine what in the content *must* be known. What is it that is essential for learners to know before leaving the session?
- Then, what else *should* they know – that is, very relevant, central information about the topic?
- Finally, what remains that they *could* know? This is what it would be good to fit in if there is time or that you could direct your learners to if they want or need to expand their knowledge.

Having sorted the content in this way, build the structure around what must be known, plan where to fit in the should be known, and be ready to use or reject the could be known according to how the session unfolds.

Question 4: How do you structure an introduction to get the maximum attention of students?

I suggested earlier that in starting a session it is important to announce the learning objectives (Question 1) and to explain the context (Question 3). It is also important to provide the outline or framework of the session. However, while it is essential to deal with the objectives, context, and outline, they may not be the best things to focus on if you wish to get learners' attention right from the start.

If you want to gain everyone's attention, here are some possibilities.

- Explain the usefulness and/or relevance of the topic.
- Be explicit about how this session links with the assessment.
- In a vocational subject, emphasize how the content will help in getting work and/or succeeding in work.
- Make an immediate connection between the content and the known or likely experience of group members.
- Convey something about your personal involvement, perspective or feelings. For example, if you experienced some strong feelings on first encountering this topic, say so: 'When I first came across this idea, I was thrilled/initially confused/fascinated'. If you are presenting a theory or model that you have strong reservations about or which you have found especially useful in your current or previous work, say so.

- If you are trying something new, tell the learners about it: 'I'm going to teach this in a different way today, I'm really keen to see how it goes and if you think it works'.
- Make a startling statement or show a startling image (relevant to the topic of course!).
- If you are using slides in the session, consider not using slides to accompany your initial words. This will assist the learners in focusing on you and what you are saying.
- Tell a (relevant) story or an anecdote. You might decide only to begin the tale and save the next part or ending until later. (You will find more on the use of stories in Question 22.)
- Ask the learners to imagine themselves in a particular situation, which then leads into the topic.
- If you are planning to use activities, use a brief activity at the beginning, one that is designed to arouse learners' interest or curiosity.

Although clarity about the objectives, the context, and the framework for the session are crucial for learners' cognitive understanding, a good introduction will hook the audience and engage the learners emotionally by engendering feelings such as curiosity, surprise, reassurance, excitement, fascination or motivation.

Task 3

Pick a session you are familiar with. Think of an anecdote you could relate in the first couple of minutes which is actually or effectively true, which is also relevant to the topic, and which is likely to leave the learners feeling intrigued.

Question 5: Should there be one standard method of teaching undergraduates?

Before offering a direct answer to this question, it is worth noting that 'teaching' is defined variously in higher education. The broadest definition would be along the following lines: 'any activity that the teacher engages in that is intended to assist students' learning', and would therefore include course and module design, assessment design, feedback, personal tutorials, and the design of online activities. Many of the current crop of 'teaching excellence' awards in higher education reflect this broad range of activities (see Question 55). Question 5, however, assumed the more conventional definition of teaching, which concentrates on what the teacher does in a room with a group of learners.

Despite the advance of online learning and even though Graham Gibbs wrote *Twenty Terrible Reasons for Lecturing* as long ago as 1981, the lecture appears to continue to hold sway as the most prevalent method for teaching in universities. I take 'lecture' to mean a teacher imparting information to a group of learners, probably with the accompaniment of PowerPoint slides or other visual aids.

The lecture is just one method of learning and teaching and many more are explored in Questions 6 and 7. The key factor that should determine the choice of method is the objectives for the session. No one method is suitable for achieving the different types of objectives.

Other factors that can exert an influence on the choice of method include:

- the size of the group;
- the time available;
- the expectations of the learners;
- direction or pressure from colleagues;
- the confidence and imagination (or lack thereof) of the teacher;
- the time that the teacher has for preparation;
- the nature of the discipline or subject.

Although the objectives might indicate that a lecture is not the most appropriate method to use, it is still often chosen, usually because of one or more of the above factors. In the first edition of *What's the Use of Lectures?*, Donald Bligh (1971) collated research from literally hundreds of sources to consider the question of what lectures could and could not achieve for learners. He has continued to update the book and it remains a comprehensive account of what research can tell us about the uses of this dominant method.

Bligh stresses that there are limitations to what the lecture can achieve. One of the key points to emerge from his work is that if you want to gain the attention of your audience, generally you should not talk at them for more than about twenty minutes.

> a combination of psychological and physiological studies using a range of criteria, together with common experience, are beginning to form a composite picture that the first 20–30 minutes of a lecture are different from the remainder. The remainder is probably less effective and less efficient.
>
> (Bligh 1998: 61)

Most lectures are scheduled to last at least forty-five minutes and often are expected to last two or even three hours. Although there are exceptional lecturers who can hold the attention of an audience for long periods and there are committed and resilient learners who will remain attentive despite the performance of the lecturer, Bligh's assertion rings true for most.

This finding is endorsed from another field. In writing on the workings of the brain, James Zull describes the phenomenon of 'habituation':

> if we hear a repeated sound for a while, it becomes mesmerizing – even tranquilizing. Eventually we begin to ignore it; we literally do not hear it. This is called *habituation* and it is a characteristic of neurons and networks of neurons. The synapses actually fire less frequently if we hear the same sound over and over. Nothing demonstrates habituation more than a lecture. Unless we break up the sound every few minutes we are almost certain to induce habituation.
>
> (Zull 2002: 149)

This key point and more of the research cited by Bligh suggests that active learning is more effective than passive learning. 'Passive' describes the behaviour of the learner who sits in a lecture and, at best, listens, reads the slides or handouts, and makes notes. The assumption is that their role in the lecture is confined to absorbing information and ideas. Learning becomes active when the learner does more than this, such as asks questions, considers alternatives or seeks to explain or compare. It is possible that this is being done silently and internally in the conventional lecture, but that will be at the initiative of the individual learner. It will depend on factors such as their ability, motivation, and style of learning. If it is happening, it will be happening despite the teaching method.

James Zull writes:

> any learning that involves some sense of progress and control by the learner might be expected to engage the basal structures. This would be learning that is pleasurable.
>
> (Zull 2002: 62)

> Poldrack and his colleagues found that activation of the basal structures occurred when the learner was engaged in postulating answers and getting feedback on them, an active learning setting. But when the learner was simply asked to memorize associations, the basal structures were less active and the back areas of cortex near the memory systems were more active.
>
> (Zull 2002: 63)

Active learning is most likely to happen when the teacher directs activities during the session, when the session departs from being merely the transmission of information. It involves activities such as questioning, debate, discussion, and application. Of course, the teacher can also deliberately encourage or direct the learners to engage in active learning outside of contact time (see Question 49).

The need for active learning is also borne out by the influential ideas of David Kolb whose *Experiential Learning* was published in 1984. Kolb drew on the work of John Dewey, Kurt Lewin, and Jean Piaget to delineate the process of learning from experience. He captured his model of experiential learning in a diagram, which, in a simplified form, has became known as 'Kolb's learning cycle' and has figured prominently in teacher training programmes in the post-compulsory sector over the last twenty-five years. Figure 1 shows how the cycle is commonly presented:

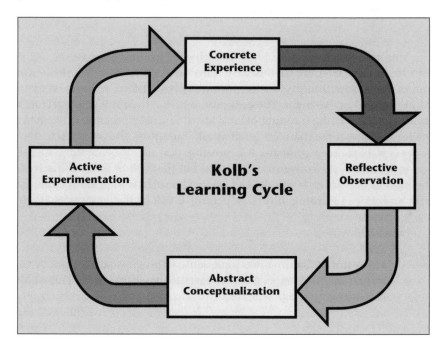

Figure 1. Kolb's learning cycle.

Whenever the cycle is explained in textbooks or in workshops, Kolb's original terms are often replaced by more everyday and often more simplistic terms, such as:

- Concrete experience = doing
- Reflective observation = reflecting or thinking
- Abstract conceptualization = theorizing, hypothesizing or concluding
- Active experimentation = planning or testing

The suggestion is that for an effective learning experience, the learner needs to go around the cycle at least once. This is what many people do naturally in their day-to-day existence without consciously thinking of the notion of a learning cycle. It describes conventional on-the-job learning. For instance, in learning about teaching, you:

- run a session – concrete experience;
- reflect on the experience afterwards – reflective observation;
- draw conclusions on the basis of your reflection about how the session could be improved – abstract conceptualization;
- begin to make plans to test out your conclusion for the next time you run the session – active experimentation;
- run the session again;
- and continue round the cycle.

This is, to many, unremarkable and has been called, 'common sense'. However, not all of your learners will be doing this and the question for you is, 'What do you do, as a lecturer, to force or at least to encourage learners to go round Kolb's learning cycle during a session or throughout a module?' If you are going to do this, key points to remember are:

- The learner can enter the cycle at any point. For instance, you could present a theory for them to test out or you could begin by asking them to reflect on their experience.
- The learner must exercise some choice and control as they progress around the cycle. It is he or she who needs to reflect, draw conclusions, plan how to test conclusions, and so on.

Learning by Doing by Graham Gibbs (1988) has many practical suggestions for activities to assist learners in navigating specific points in the cycle. The book is out of print but the full text can be found at: http://www2.glos.ac.uk/gdn/gibbs/index.htm.

There is no standard method of teaching undergraduates and the most common form – the lecture – is best seen as just one option. It is important for you as a teacher to:

- develop a repertoire of methods to use;
- be able to choose the most appropriate methods for the circumstances;
- use those methods effectively.

Guidance on a range of methods is provided in Questions 6 and 7.

Question 6: What can you do with 100 students in an amphitheatre besides lecture?

The case is made in Question 5 that lecturing for all of the time is not the only option, even when the size of the group and the layout of the room are among the factors that make you come to the conclusion that there is no alternative. There are many activities that you can use instead of or alongside lecturing. Here are ten ideas for breaking up a lecture, all but one (the round) suitable with groups of any size.

1. *Buzz groups*. Intermittently throughout the lecture, ask learners to talk briefly in groups of two or three, for just two or three minutes, to yield opinions or to answer a question.
2. *Application*. For example, you could say to the learners, 'Look at this case and state how you would apply the idea/approach I have just outlined'.
3. *Review*. Stop the lecture for five minutes and ask learners, in groups of two or three, to look through their notes and review and summarize the lecture up to this point or pick out what for them is the most important or striking thing.
4. *Problem-solving*. Present a practical problem for learners to tackle for a few minutes, individually or in pairs.
5. *Plan*. Ask learners to plan what they need to do next to use the information from the session or to learn more about the topic.
6. *Handouts/worksheets*. These can be used in different ways to break the flow of a lecture. You could:

   - Distribute handouts that follow the structure of the lecture but which include exercises in which learners have to answer a question, record a response, add to graphics, etc.
   - Include a brief piece for learners to read. Ask them to pick out what for them is the most important or most striking point about the passage and discuss this with the person sitting next to them. This could lead into the next part of the lecture.
   - Ask the learners to work through a series of questions on a worksheet at the end of the lecture, which acts as an informal test of their recall and understanding.

   More detail on different uses of handouts can be found in Question 39.
7. *Question-asking*. See Question 18.
8. *Quizzes*. Break up the lecture with a short quiz so as to recap on key points and provoke discussion. The quiz can be conducted in teams

and it may be verbal or written. It can also be used as an introduction. You may be able to use keypads (see Question 21) for this.

9. *Round.* This technique can be used midway through or at the end of a session. It is suitable for groups of up to around thirty. Each person in the group repeats out loud the start of a sentence and then completes it. For example, (midway) 'So far I have found this topic …', or (end) 'As a result of today's session, I …' or 'The main point I am taking away from this session is …'. Anyone who does not for any reason want to contribute just says, 'Pass'. It takes two to three minutes to hear everyone do this with a group of thirty.

10. *Rest.* Of course, you can always just have a break to stretch legs and chat.

More ideas for taking brief breaks in lectures can be found in *Practical Ideas for Enhancing Lectures* by Peter Davies (2003).

Other methods commonly used within a lecture include:

*   *Listening to an audio recording or viewing a video recording.* This might be done with a list of questions or headings under which learners should make notes (see Question 14).
*   *Case study.* The details of a real or simulated set of circumstances or problem are presented (either verbally or by a handout) to learners for them to consider possible responses or solutions.
*   *Demonstration.* Showing the group how to perform a practical task, usually with clearly defined stages and usually followed by the opportunity for practice.
*   *Panel/witness group.* A number of group members or specialist guests respond to questions or hold a discussion in front of the group.

Task 4
If you wrote an objective for Task 1, return to it and list which of the methods above would be best suited to help your learners achieve that objective.

Question 7: If you are in a situation where your teaching consists of lecturing to large groups of students, how do you provide opportunities for them to apply principles, analyse, evaluate, and synthesize?

This question referred to Bloom's taxonomy, which had been discussed earlier in the session. In *Taxonomy of Educational Objectives (Book 1: Cognitive Domain),*

Benjamin Bloom and his colleagues categorized different levels of cognitive activity, 'intended to provide for classification of the goals of our educational system' (Bloom 1956: 1). Later volumes extended the taxonomy to include the affective domain and the psychomotor domain. The taxonomy was revised by Lorin Anderson, David Krathwohl, and others in 2001.

The taxonomy for the cognitive domain has proved enduringly useful for teachers in all contexts when they come to articulate what it is they want their learners to achieve. In higher education, it is used to assist in identifying session objectives or module learning outcomes. Bloom's original six categories of the cognitive domain were knowledge, comprehension, application, analysis, synthesis, and evaluation. These are listed in ascending order of cognitive difficulty. The following are the kinds of activities learners are expected to engage in at each of these levels:

- *Knowledge*: define, duplicate, label, list, memorize, name, order, recognize, recall, repeat, reproduce, state, tell.
- *Comprehension*: classify, describe, discuss, explain, identify, indicate, locate, report, review, select.
- *Application*: apply, demonstrate, employ, operate, practise, schedule, solve, use.
- *Analysis*: analyse, calculate, categorize, compare, contrast, criticize, differentiate, discriminate, distinguish, examine, experiment, question, test, inspect, debate.
- *Synthesis*: compose, construct, create, design, develop, formulate, propose, set up.
- *Evaluation*: appraise, argue, assess, choose, defend, judge, predict, rate, select, support, evaluate.

Question 7 follows the suggestion that the conventional lecture is likely to assist learning only at the lower end of the taxonomy – that is, acquiring knowledge and developing comprehension. These are reproductive activities and are sometimes encouraged by assessment tasks at these two levels, which test the learners' ability to recall and recite the facts or theories that they have learnt. If the lecture method consists of the teacher offering information to learners, the learners are being expected to do little beyond absorb and remember that information.

The question asks how can the opportunities for activity at the higher levels of the taxonomy be encouraged, if not demanded, in a session. Another question captured this problem by asking,

> 'Even if lectures are limited in what they are likely to achieve, should a lecture aim to achieve a "productive" outcome (application, analysis,

synthesis, etc.) or should it just aim "low", i.e. for the "reproductive outcome"?'

The answer is the same as in Question 5, 'ensure your methods match the objectives'. So, if one of your objectives for the session is

'Create a set of criteria to assess Home Office interpretation of immigration rules',

you should arrange for the learners to engage in an activity that is likely to make them better equipped to create such criteria. You can choose from the activities that follow or from those listed in Question 6 to identify one or more suitable activities for helping learners achieve the objective. This reinforces the point that while lectures have their uses, they are limited. If you want to help learners achieve objectives across the full range of Bloom's taxonomy, you need to draw on a variety of techniques.

At this point, it is useful to look at the detail of the revised taxonomy produced by Anderson, Krathwohl, and others (2001) in Table 1. The principal changes to the original taxonomy are to use verbs to describe each level and to switch the order of 'evaluation' and 'synthesis', now known as 'evaluate' and 'create'. You can use the 'cognitive processes' column to help you clarify what you want the learners to do and use it as a basis for determining the most suitable method.

Table 1. The cognitive process dimension: categories and cognitive processes

Category	Cognitive processes	Definitions
Remember – to retrieve relevant knowledge from long-term memory		
	Recognizing	Locating knowledge in long-term memory that is consistent with presented material
	Recalling	Retrieving relevant knowledge from long-term memory
Understand – to construct meaning from instructional messages, including oral, written, and graphic communication		
	Interpreting	Changing from one form of representation (e.g. numerical) to another (e.g. verbal)
	Exemplifying	Finding a specific example or illustration of a concept or principle
	Classifying	Determining that something belongs to a category
	Summarizing	Abstracting a general theme or major point

(Continued)

Table 1. (*continued*)

Category	Cognitive processes	Definitions
	Inferring	Drawing a logical conclusion from presented information
	Comparing	Detecting correspondences between two ideas, objects, and the like
	Explaining	Constructing a cause-and-effect model of a system

Apply – to carry out or use a procedure in a given situation

	Executing	Applying a procedure to a familiar task
	Implementing	Applying a procedure to an unfamiliar task

Analyse – to break material into its constituent parts and determine how the parts relate to one another and to an overall structure or purpose

	Differentiating	Distinguishing relevant from irrelevant parts or important from unimportant parts of presented material
	Organizing	Determining how elements fit or function within a structure
	Attributing	Determining a point of view, bias, values or intent underlying presented material

Evaluate – to make judgements based on criteria and standards

	Checking	Detecting inconsistencies or fallacies within a process or product; determining whether a process or product has internal consistency; detecting the effectiveness of a procedure as it is being implemented
	Critiquing	Detecting inconsistencies between a product and external criteria; determining whether a product has external consistency; detecting the appropriateness of a procedure for a given problem

Create – to put elements together to form a coherent or functional whole; to reorganize elements into a new pattern or structure

	Generating	Coming up with alternative hypotheses based on criteria
	Planning	Devising a procedure for accomplishing some task
	Producing	Inventing a product

Adapted from table 5.1 in Anderson, L.W. and Krathwohl, D.R. (eds.) (2001) *A Taxonomy for Learning, Teaching, and Assessing: A Revision of Bloom's Taxonomy of Educational Objectives.* New York: Longman.

Many teachers say they use the lecture to provide learners with information and leave them to do the analysis, application, and so on afterwards. Three objections to this are:

1. The learners will not necessarily go away and engage in that behaviour, so one needs to consider directed activities outside of the lecture theatre (see Question 49).
2. Given what was said in Question 5, the learners will be inattentive and not gather information for the best part of the session.
3. Learners are more likely to recall and remember by immediately working with that knowledge: applying, analysing, and so on makes recall more likely (see 'the value of rehearsal' in Question 13).

On some undergraduate courses, the lowest two levels of Bloom's taxonomy are all that are tackled in the first year of a three-year course. In the second year levels three and four are addressed, and in the third year levels five and six. Imagine the effect of this on first-year students – a whole year when they are expected to do nothing more than to retain information without having the chance to apply it, explore it or work with it in some way. If you want learners to be more motivated in a session and to have a better chance of remembering information from that session, ensure they have the opportunity to operate at more than the lowest levels of Bloom's taxonomy.

Remember also that the taxonomy is in ascending order of difficulty; this does not prevent you asking your learners to pursue further complexity within a topic at each of the six levels. This is shown in Figure 2.

Question 7 used the term 'large groups'. What follows are seven activities that could be used with groups of varying sizes but less than the hundred specified in Question 6. For each activity, the optimum size of group with which it might work is indicated. All seven activities are designed to promote active and interactive learning and are suited to the higher levels of Bloom's taxonomy referred to in the question.

Activity 1: Pyramids

This is an example of how a pyramid (sometimes called a snowball) works.

Stage 1. Provide learners with a task to do individually for one minute. For example:

*   What do you think are the three most important points from the last section of the lecture?
*   Make two suggestions as to how you would solve the problem presented.

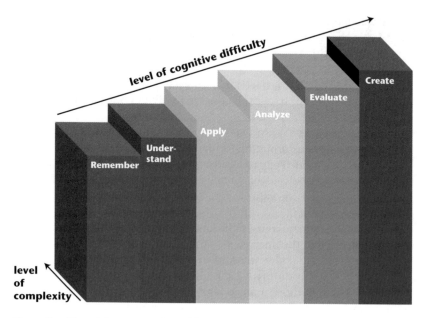

Figure 2. Bloom's taxonomy of cognitive activity.

- Suggest three responses you might make in the scenario I have just outlined.

Stage 2. Individuals form pairs and they have two minutes to listen to what the other has come up with and to agree on their joint response.

Stage 3. Pairs form groups of four and have three minutes to agree on their joint response.

Stage 4. Fours form groups of eight and have three minutes to agree and appoint one person ready to announce what they have agreed as a group.

Stage 5. At this point you may want to hear briefly from each group of eight and comment on or record their suggestions. In a sense, what you do at this point is less important than in previous stages because everyone, however large the group, will have had to talk and be actively involved in the task.

For this method to be effective:

- Make sure the task is simple and clearly explained – this is more important the bigger the group.

- Choose an amount of time for each stage (the times above are examples) that will allow for thought and discussion but not take too long.
- Manage the formation of groups when the total numbers prevent a 1–2–4–8 progression, just to ensure the groups do not become too unwieldy.

This can work with groups of up to about eighty.

Activity 2: Fishbowl

This activity is suited to sessions in which you want learners to articulate their own point of view and to explore competing arguments or perspectives. It requires a group of between ten and thirty and a room with some flexibility in the seating.

To set it up:

- arrange four, five or six chairs in a circle;
- invite learners to sit in the chairs;
- explain the rules;
- present the question;
- begin.

This is how it operates. The people in the circle of chairs debate the question. The remaining members of the group stand around the circle, listening to the debate. If anyone from the rest of the group wants to contribute, they tap one of the people in the seats and take their place. The one who was seated becomes part of the larger group.

You may want to add some extra rules, such as once you have been tapped out you cannot go back in. You may prefer the rest of the group to be seated rather than standing, although people will be more likely to tap in if they are standing. When this works well, teachers report that it enlivens the session and absorbs the whole group, and often learners who have never spoken before join in. It can also ensure that individuals do not dominate a discussion as they can be tapped out. It can be used to follow up information you have provided or as the introduction to a topic, leading into more information from you or, for example, the investigation of a case study.

To make it more likely to work, select the topic carefully. Be wary of the topic or the phrasing of the question leading to consensus or agreement – debate is essential for the activity to engage everyone. Stick to just four, five or six in the group. Too few makes for less disagreement, too many means some in the circle may not get the chance to speak. Be ready if necessary to steer the discussion back on track to the prescribed topic. You will need to decide how long the fishbowl should last; if learners become very involved, you may need to intervene to stop it. Equally, if it does not start well, be ready to tap yourself in to take on a role and provoke some response.

The fishbowl lends itself to subjects where there is no 'right' answer, where it is important for learners to explore alternative, competing viewpoints and to establish their own position. It can work with groups of up to thirty.

Activity 3: Line up

This is another device that is useful for getting learners to articulate their position on a given issue. It can also energize learners through movement and can have the same effect as an icebreaker (see Question 9), which is topic related.

This activity involves asking learners to stand in a line. Where they stand in the line will reflect their stance on a question. You provide the statement, such as 'Free healthcare should not be available for lifelong smokers with smoking-related illnesses'. Ask learners to stand at one end if they 'wholly agree', at the other end if they 'wholly disagree', or at the appropriate spot in between. The crucial thing is to get learners to check with those on either side of them if they are in the right position relative to each other on the statement. In other words, every learner will have to talk about the topic very briefly. This can be done with very large groups but that will depend on the size of the room and the flexibility of furniture in it. If you do try this, please note that you will almost certainly not get a line. It is more likely to look like a collection of clusters or small groups. With some undergraduate learners, it is worth stressing that you are not looking for a right answer.

Variations include:

- Asking learners to rate their position on a numerical scale where, for example, 1 = 'wholly agree' and 10 = 'wholly disagree', before standing up.
- Modifying the statement after the initial line-up and asking learners where they would stand now.
- Repeating the initial statement/line-up at the end of the session, giving learners a chance to see if they have changed their position and perhaps to explain their movement/non-movement to another.

As an opening to a session that is about learners engaging with a contentious issue, this can be a good way to get everyone talking. The technique has been used successfully as a prelude to a fishbowl exercise (above), by taking, say, two learners from one end of the line, two from the other end, and one from the middle to start the fishbowl, thereby ensuring a range of opinion for the fishbowl discussion. The number of people who can participate in a line-up is restricted only by the amount of space available for a line.

Activity 4: Five minutes each way

This activity ensures that everyone in the group gets the chance to speak. It can be used with groups of all sizes. Ask learners to sit or stand in pairs. Each pair of learners should face each other. For the first part of the exercise, A talks to B for a fixed time, say five minutes. In the second part of the exercise, B talks to A for the same amount of time. You indicate what they should talk about, for example, 'what I have learned from this session', 'the key points for me are as follows' or 'these are the questions I am left with after this session'. The listener should only listen. They should not interrupt their partner other than to show they are being attentive or, if necessary, to stop the speaker straying from the topic at hand.

What this exercise does is to get each person in the group to think out loud, uninterrupted, for the five minutes (you may decide two minutes is more practical). For many learners, this is a challenge. For some it is a treat, as to have someone's undivided, impartial attention for five minutes is an experience they rarely, if ever, have enjoyed. It is most likely to be used at the end of a session, as a form of review or reflection or as a means of planning. It is an excellent vehicle for rehearsal (see Question 13). It is not intended that you in any way monitor or require feedback from the exercise. An incidental effect of the exercise is that the listener can practise the discipline of being attentive and not interrupting.

Like a pyramid, this activity should work with groups of up to about eighty.

Activity 5: Solvit

This activity assumes each person has their own problem to solve or question to answer when they are working, for example, on individually negotiated projects or assignments.

Learners assemble in groups of five or six. One person starts as the 'presenter', that is, the one who presents their problem. Another person is the recorder – the one who is going to record accepted suggestions. The presenter presents their problem in the form of a question, which the recorder writes down, preferably on a flip chart for all members of the group to see. The recorder and other members of the group can ask the presenter to clarify aspects of the problem but cannot yet make any suggestions for solutions. Once the problem has been fully heard and understood, then group members can suggest how to solve the problem. The group does not debate any suggestions; they are simply called out. In response to each suggestion, the presenter accepts it as worth exploring later – in which case the recorder writes it underneath the question – or (politely) rejects it and waits for the next suggestion. Eventually the presenter has a list of a few potentially useful ideas for them to take away and use as the basis for planning their solution or next step. The group then continues with a new presenter and new recorder and so on until everyone has taken the role of presenter and has received a few useful suggestions. Assuming that there are no rigid seating arrangements as in a lecture theatre, fifty might be the maximum number for which this activity could operate effectively.

Activity 6: Crossover

See Question 20.

Activity 7: Poster tour

See Question 33.

Of course, in very practical subjects, if the numbers allow, there is also the option for learners to practise a clearly defined task, preferably with instant feedback from you or their peers, or with the use of a checklist for self-assessment. What would be really beneficial is if you can make and play back a video recording of the learner's performance, critically appraising this with the aid of their peers.

Question 8: How many learning techniques should I use in a two-hour lecture with 110 adult learners?

This is a precise question looking for a precise answer. However, it would be unwise to prescribe a formula for the number of activities based on the period of time available and the number of learners.

A better way to approach this question is as follows. When planning a session, list which behaviours you are expecting the learners to be engaged in at different stages. For example:

2.00	Listening to me and taking notes
2.15	Discussing in groups of three
2.25	Listening to comments from other learners, perhaps making comments themselves
2.40	Watching a DVD
3.00	Listening to me and taking notes again
3.15	Break, and so on

When you have created the list, check to ensure that:

- all of the learner behaviours are designed to achieve the objectives;
- there are no excessively long periods of passivity for the learners;

- there is no over-reliance on any one method – there are few things worse as a learner than being told for the fifth time in a session, 'now get in groups and discuss your response to what I have just told you'.

Task 5

Look back on the last session you ran. Can you list the different behaviours you expected learners to engage in? Check them against the three bullet points above.

Question 9: What are effective icebreakers for new groups to foster future effective group interactive learning?

An icebreaker is an activity that takes place near the beginning of a session with the intention of making the learners feel at ease and giving them the chance to hear from other group members. It is most usually used when the group is meeting for the first time. Icebreakers are easier and more suitable with smaller groups of up to twenty, but some may be used successfully with larger groups.

The following is an example of an icebreaker:

> It is the first meeting of the group of 12 learners. The teacher has spent ten minutes introducing details of the course. The teacher says:
> 'I would like you to sit with someone you have not met before today. Spend a few minutes talking with them and find out four things:
>
> 1. Their name
> 2. How they came to be on the course
> 3. What they are hoping to get from the course
> 4. One other thing about them*
>
> Take a few minutes to find these things out and make sure you are ready to introduce your partner to the rest of the group'.

(* You need to decide on whether to specify this 'one other thing' or leave it open. This will depend on what kind of climate you want to create. In some circumstances, it would be appropriate to specify things such as favourite TV programme or website, last book you read, hobby, special interest. Or it may be suitable to make it study related – the last module you took, anything you already know about this topic. If you want it to be perhaps a little more personal, try:

- Which famous person, living or dead, would you most like to be stuck in a lift with?

- If you were wearing a T-shirt with a few words on, what would those words be, which summed up your outlook?
- What would be your perfect day?
- What would you normally be doing at this time of the day on this day of the week?/What were you doing this time last week?)

When the few minutes are up, the teacher asks each person in turn to introduce their partner briskly to the rest of the group. You can adapt this example. You might ask each person to introduce themselves in turn to the whole group, saying those four things. However, this has the potential with some groups of learners to make them feel more anxious than relaxed.

In a large group, you could start the activity in the same way, but instead of each person introducing their partner to the whole group, pairs form fours and each person introduces their partner to the new pair.

An icebreaker should achieve the following:

1. Exchange information between group members, including the teacher.
2. Create a warm climate/set the right tone.
3. Give learners a chance to talk and to get involved from the beginning.
4. Give learners the opportunity to hear their voice in the presence of the whole group.

The example above should achieve all of these. The overall effect is for the learners to feel more relaxed and more ready to learn.

Sometimes, however, an icebreaker can turn into an *icemaker*. The following are ways in which intended icebreakers can have the opposite effect:

- the task asks the learners to reveal or say something they may feel awkward or uncomfortable about;
- the task provides the opportunity for some learners to fail or visibly perform less well than others;
- the directions for the task are unclear;
- the activity takes too long and/or one or more learners take much more time over their introductions;
- learners don't see any point in the activity.

Another effective icebreaker is 'People Bingo'. Each person is given a bingo card, say a sheet of A4 paper with boxes on. Each of the boxes has a phrase written in it, such as:

- has been on holiday to Cornwall
- speaks a second language
- was born in June

- is a collector
- lives in (nearby town)
- wears contact lenses

Each person has to mix with the rest of the group and find people who fit the descriptions in the boxes. They can put just one name in each box. Notionally there is a winner – the first person to find people who fit all the boxes – but what really happens is that everyone gets absorbed in conversation with each other about the items in the boxes. If you can include some questions related to the module content, all for the better.

You can also use the model of the line-up (see Question 7) as an icebreaker, although instead of using the line-up to find out people's opinions and attitudes, the line can be of a factual nature, for example, stand in order of:

- first names, alphabetically
- birthdates in the year
- how far you have travelled

and everyone is encouraged to talk with those on either side of them.

Here is one for use in a small group and with a brave teacher. Each person introduces themselves to the whole group and ends their introduction with a question directed at the teacher, about the teacher, and which the teacher then answers.

The best icebreakers will simultaneously achieve the four targets in the numbered list above and also introduce the topic. When running workshops on the topic of 'Teaching with Emotional Intelligence' for teachers at university, I often ask each participant at the start to recall an episode when they were a learner that aroused strong feelings in them and then to spend two or three minutes exchanging their recollection with one other. I ask people to volunteer specific brief information about their tale to the whole group and this leads into my introduction to the topic. This whole section takes five to ten minutes. It (usually) works well in serving the function of an icebreaker and also provides a starting point for the topic.

Question 10: Is it important to give background information about yourself with reference to knowledge and experience, and does this affect the audience's perception of your credibility?

Your credibility in your subject should be evidenced by your knowledge and confidence in relation to the subject. If you want to confirm your experience and background with your audience before you begin, be wary of appearing to justify yourself too much and setting yourself up to be tested beyond your reach.

You may vary the emphasis on different aspects of your credibility according to the audience: an audience of researchers is likely to want to know about your research credentials; an audience of practitioners is more likely to be reassured about your experience in practice.

If you do not set out to establish your credibility at the start you can seek to do so incidentally, but possibly deliberately, during the session, such as when using examples from your research or experience to illustrate a point.

Question 11: How to increase/stimulate the learner wanting/needing?

This question followed after a brief introduction to Phil Race's model of learning. Simply put, Phil Race suggests that a learner needs to experience five things for learning to be effective, especially during a complete module or programme but if possible during a single session:

- opportunities for learning by *doing* – practice, trial and error;
- *feedback* on their progress and understanding;
- time to *digest* the content of the learning;
- *wanting* to learn;
- *needing* to learn.

Race has based a book on this idea – *Making Learning Happen* (2005). In a second edition of the book, due to be published in 2010, he adds two further components:

- the chance to *teach* others;
- the chance to *assess* themselves and others.

Wanting is the equivalent of intrinsic motivation – interest in the subject and in the session. Needing can be characterized as extrinsic motivation – seeing the point of the learning and anticipating the reward that will follow from successful learning. A learner may bring either or both of intrinsic and extrinsic motivation with them and this helps the learning greatly. However, it is important for you to consider how to plan to stimulate both in your group.

Extrinsic motivation is the more straightforward to deal with. You can explain to the learner why the topic is being studied, how it fits into the module, and how it will be useful to them in their future studies and career. The most potent form of extrinsic motivation for most learners is knowing how a session links to their assessment. Many lecturers bemoan the fact that their learners appear to make an effort only if they can see an explicit link between their endeavours and an assessment. However, if you are interested in influencing learner behaviour, then recognizing that assessment is likely to be the key driver of that behaviour is an invaluable piece of knowledge. There is more information on this in Question 44.

How can you develop intrinsic motivation in the learner in your session? The enthusiasm, expertise, and vitality that you put into your explanations may not be enough, so make sure that the tasks they have to complete are relevant, achievable and, hopefully, absorbing. Some examples of such tasks are given later in this answer.

When thinking about learner motivation, it is time to face up to a fact that causes gloom among many teachers in higher education:

> to view the 'impact' or 'effectiveness' of teaching solely in terms of teaching methods or the quality of their execution by lecturers … is narrow and inadequate. Student learning is subject to a dynamic and richly complex array of influences … This web of influences spans assessment procedures and course content and structure as well as teaching.
>
> (Marton et al. 1997: 253)

However resourceful, dynamic, imaginative or just simply great you are in the classroom or lecture theatre, you are not the sole or perhaps even the most important influence on the learning and motivation of learners. This is explored fully in texts that address the notion of learners' approaches to learning, which has been very influential in learning and teaching in higher education in recent years. It began with the work of Ference Marton and Roger Saljo (Marton and Saljo 1976a, 1976b) in Sweden and was developed by Noel Entwistle and Paul Ramsden in the UK (Entwistle and Ramsden 1983) and by John Biggs from Australia (Biggs 1987). The suggestion initially was that learners in higher education were capable of adopting either a 'deep' or 'surface' approach to their learning. A learner's approach to a learning task determined their degree of engagement, which in turn shaped the outcomes of the learning.

A deep approach indicates an intention to understand ideas, to make sense of the subject, to develop an interest in the subject itself and a desire to learn. Learners who adopt a deep approach follow up their own interests even if these are outside those parts of the course that are assessed.

A deep approach involves:

- relating ideas to previous knowledge and experience;
- looking for patterns and underlying principles;
- checking evidence and relating it to conclusions;

- examining logic and argument cautiously and critically;
- becoming actively interested in the course content.

(Marton et al. 1997: 19)

In contrast, a surface approach indicates an intention to cope with course requirements. Learners who adopt this approach attempt to memorize subject matter and are not interested in studying a subject for its own sake. They keep narrowly to the syllabus as laid down in course descriptions and do not follow up interests of their own (if they have any).

A surface approach involves:

- studying without reflecting on either purpose or strategy;
- treating the course as unrelated bits of knowledge;
- memorizing facts and procedures routinely;
- finding difficulty in making sense of new ideas presented;
- feeling undue pressure and worry about work.

(ibid)

The learning that results from a deep approach is more likely to endure.

The idea of a strategic or achieving approach was proposed by John Biggs (1987). This indicates an intention to achieve the highest possible grades, well-organized study methods, and competitiveness. Learners who adopt a strategic approach are oriented towards doing well, whatever that requires.

A strategic or achieving approach involves:

- putting consistent effort into studying;
- finding the right conditions and materials for study;
- managing time and effort effectively;
- being alert to assessment requirements and criteria;
- gearing work to the perceived preferences of lecturers.

(ibid)

If you think of the strategic approach as always working in combination with one of the other two approaches, there are four different combinations of approaches adopted by learners:

- strategic and deep
- strategic and surface
- non-strategic and deep
- non-strategic and surface
  (see Figure 3)

Clearly, some of the characteristics of the surface and strategic approaches as outlined above do not go together. The strategic/surface combination would

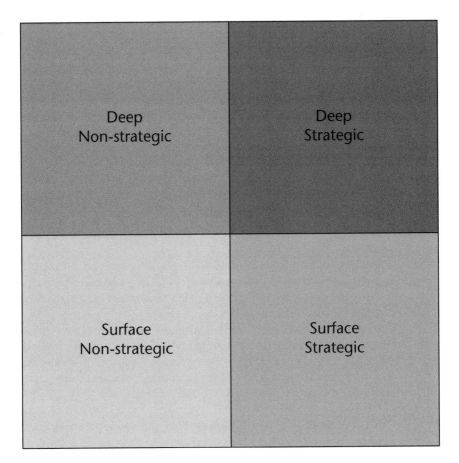

Figure 3. Four combinations of approaches that learners might adopt.

mean a learner strategically adopting a surface approach, such as memorizing facts without looking for meaning because the learner knows that is what will be rewarded.

The questioner asked about 'wanting' and 'needing'. It would be difficult to adopt a deep approach to learning without intrinsic motivation – wanting to learn. At the same time, learners who adopt a strategic approach to learning are driven by extrinsic motivation – needing to learn. So to 'increase/stimulate wanting/needing' as the question asks, it would be worth investigating the factors that influence learners' approaches to learning and to identify those which stimulate a deep or strategic approach.

There are things that learners bring with them to their studies that affect their approach to learning and motivation to learn: their ability, their reasons for being there, and their previous experience of learning. But the key point to remember is that the approach to and motivation for learning are not fixed. In the context in which learning takes place, some factors can exert a strong influence both on which approach is adopted and on the learner's motivation. Some of these factors are determined at the course design stage and you may not be in a position to influence them. As Toohey says:

> The elements which enable deep learning must be built into the design of the course. If they are not, individual teachers, however creative they may be, will always be struggling to overcome the structural limitations of the course.
>
> (Toohey 1999: 18)

These factors include:

- *The quantity of material in the curriculum.* Focusing on the transmission and recall of excessive content is likely to induce a surface approach. It is important to 'emphasize depth of learning rather than breadth of coverage' (Biggs and Tang 2007: 25).
- *The quality and frequency of feedback available to learners.* Feedback has been identified as the most potent factor influencing learner achievement (Hattie 2003). Consider three aspects of feedback: its quality, its frequency, and the extent to which the learner is assisted in or encouraged to hear or read it, understand it, and act on it.
- *The nature of the assessment tasks.* Assessment tasks that emphasize recall over understanding are more likely to induce a surface approach.
- *The extent to which learners can exert choice over their studies,* including methods of learning, content, and the nature of assessment.

There are some factors that you can influence in your face-to-face encounters with learners. John Biggs and Catherine Tang suggest:

- teaching in such a way as to explicitly bring out the structure of the topic or subject;
- teaching to elicit an active response from students, e.g. by questioning, presenting problems, rather than teaching to expound information;
- teaching by building on what students already know;
- confronting and eradicating students' misconceptions;
- teaching in a way that encourages a positive working atmosphere, so students can make mistakes and learn from them;
- using teaching methods that support the explicit aims and intended outcomes of the course.

(adapted from Biggs and Tang 2007: 25)

In addition, you can:

- use sessions to ensure clarity about the assessment requirements;
- attend to the classroom climate.

Lewis Elton has highlighted the importance of being very clear about what the assessment requires (see Question 44). Given the likelihood that learners will be driven by assessment, consider activities related to the assessment that can be used in class to develop extrinsic motivation in the learners. For example, if the assessment includes a piece of written work, perhaps an essay, a report or a project, you could try the following:

> Retain, with the students' permission, anonymized copies of work from previous groups. Introduce the students to the assessment criteria for the task and ask them, in small groups, to apply the criteria to work from previous years. You could ask them to provide a grade and be ready to justify it and perhaps even indicate what written feedback ought to include.

Such an exercise will help learners to develop a strategic approach, and develop extrinsic motivation because they should have a fuller understanding of the criteria. At the same time, the exercise should develop critical skills in the learners.

Biggs and Tang stress the importance of the learning climate, which affects 'how we and our students feel about learning. This naturally has strong effects on students' learning' (Biggs and Tang 2007: 37). I have written elsewhere (Mortiboys 2002, 2005) about the importance of attending to the emotional dimension of learning and teaching. This includes putting some energy into establishing the kind of emotional climate described above. Factors that affect the climate include:

- the extent to which you acknowledge individuals and their contributions;
- if and how you acknowledge and respond to your learners' expectations;
- how you handle learners' comments and questions;
- your use of listening skills (see Question 23);
- your non-verbal communication;
- your readiness to read and respond to learners' reactions in the classroom.

In *Classroom Assessment Techniques*, Thomas Angelo and Patricia Cross (1993) present a wealth of tasks that are often brief but demanding to ask of learners in a session as well as tasks to be undertaken in between sessions and for assessments. Here are some of their suggestions for classroom tasks that encourage deeper approaches to learning through the process of asking appropriate questions and persuading the learners to put their thoughts into words. I hope these will encourage you to investigate this resource further.

One-sentence summaries
Description: Challenge your learners to summarize a large amount of information about a given topic in one sentence.
Purpose: A technique for helping learners to grasp complex ideas by explaining them to others in non-technical language.

Directed paraphrasing
Description: An extension of the 'one-sentence summary'. Learners are challenged to produce a two- to three-paragraph summary to translate highly specialized information into language that clients/customers will understand.
Purpose: To help learners internalize their learning. Paraphrasing for a specific, non-technical audience makes the task more demanding.

Problem recognition tasks
Description: Challenge your learners to recognize and identify various types of problem in a particular field of study.
Purpose: To encourage your learners to recognize and diagnose problems first rather than trying to solve them immediately.

What's the principle?
Description: Challenge your learners to identify what type of problem they are dealing with and what principle or principles to apply to solve their problem.
Purpose: Helps your learners to recognize the general types of problems they can solve with particular principles.

Word journal
Description: Learners are expected to read given texts, journal articles, and so on in their own time. Each piece of text has to be summarized in a single word. The learner then has to write one to two paragraphs explaining why they have chosen that particular word. Learners maintain their word journal throughout the module.
Purpose: To improve learners' ability to read deeply and carefully.

Analytic memos
Description: An extension of 'directed paraphrasing'. In this case, learners are challenged to write a one- or two-page analysis of a specific problem or issue.

The person for whom the memo is written is usually a 'client' or 'employee' who needs the analysis to inform decision-making.

Purpose: Helps learners to describe and understand their problem-solving methods.

Content, form, and function outlines

Description: Learners are asked to read a poem, newspaper article, critical essay, etc. They are then asked to write brief notes under three headings: (1) What (content); (2) How (form); (3) Why (function).

Purpose: To develop learners' skills in separating and analysing the information content, the form, and the communicative function of a message.

Student-generated test questions

Description: Learners prepare test questions and model answers.

Purpose: Helps to develop skills in questioning what they are studying at a deep level.

Documented problem solutions

Description: Learners are encouraged to keep track of the steps they take in solving a problem.

Purpose: Helps learners to describe and understand their problem-solving methods.

Question 12: Which should take priority – giving the learner the tools to gain knowledge or trying to give that knowledge?

This apparently simple question does not lend itself to a straightforward answer.

The first problem is the notion that you can 'give knowledge' to the learner. This presumably means transmitting information to the learner, by talking or giving reading material or directing them to websites. There is no doubt that you can *offer* knowledge to the learner. Whether the learner receives it and does anything with it is another matter.

'Constructivism' is the concept that holds that knowledge is not just received but is constructed. In other words, for a learner to 'know' something, they have to make sense of it themselves. Individual learners bring different experiences, motivations, and intentions to bear on new knowledge that they encounter. They therefore make their own personal meaning. This means that the same piece of knowledge offered to, say, five learners, will be received and then constructed in five different ways. It is as though to make it meaningful, it has to be 'translated' by each of them into their own context or framework of existing knowledge (see Question 50).

The other part of the question refers to 'giving the learner tools to gain knowledge'. If you accept the idea of constructivism, then this is a way of describing what the effective teacher should do. If you recognize that the learner has to manipulate the knowledge that has been offered, then one task of the teacher is to assist the learner in making sense of the new knowledge. One obvious way to do this is through the kinds of in-class tasks that you ask learners to tackle.

So perhaps this question could be reworded to 'Is it enough to offer learners knowledge or should I go further and give them help in making sense of it for themselves?'

Clearly, any answer to this question implies a role for the teacher and a role for the learner. Here are four ways to help you explore your current concepts of the role of teacher and learner.

First, Paul Ramsden suggests three theories of teaching: 'three generic ways of understanding the role of the teacher in higher education, each of which has corresponding implications for how students are expected to learn' (Ramsden 2003: 108).

- *Theory 1: Teaching as telling or transmission.* Teaching is about transmitting knowledge; learning is about acquiring knowledge. Learning is separate from teaching.
- *Theory 2: Teaching as organizing student activity.* There is an association between teaching and learning. Any problems with learning can be fixed by better management of student activity.
- *Theory 3: Teaching as making learning possible.* Learning is a long and uncertain process of changes in understanding. The activities of teaching are context related, uncertain, and continuously improvable.

    (adapted from Ramsden 2003: 17–18, 108–112)

Second, John Biggs and Catherine Tang suggest three levels of teaching that teachers hold at different points in their career. They are characterized by the teacher's focus.

- *Level 1 focus: What the student is.* Teaching is 'transmitting information, usually by lecturing ... differences in learning are due to differences between students.
- *Level 2 focus: What the teacher does.* Teaching is based on 'transmitting concepts and understanding, not just information'; 'there may be more effective ways of teaching than what one is currently doing'; 'learning is seen as more of a function of what the teacher is doing, than of what sort of student one has to deal with'.
- *Level 3 focus: What the student does.* Teachers need to be clear about:

- what it means to 'understand' content in the way this is stipulated in the intended learning outcomes;
- what kind of teaching/learning activities are required to achieve those stipulated levels of understanding.

(Biggs and Tang 2007: 16–19)

Third, the Teaching Perspectives Inventory provides an online questionnaire that you can complete to find your profile in relation to five different perspectives on good teaching. Completers of the questionnaire usually find they hold one or two of the dominant perspectives. The perspectives are as follows:

- *Transmission*. Effective teaching requires a substantial commitment to the content or subject matter.
- *Apprenticeship*. Effective teaching is the process of socializing students into new behavioural norms and ways of working.
- *Developmental*. Effective teaching must be planned and conducted from the learner's point of view.
- *Nurturing*. Effective teaching assumes that long-term, hard, persistent effort to achieve comes from the heart not the head.
- *Social reform*. Effective teaching seeks to change society in substantive ways.

(details can be found at: http://www.one45.com/teachingperspectives/)

Finally, metaphors can assist you in thinking through the respective roles of you and your learners. For instance, many teachers see themselves as being the equivalent of a 'gardener to plants'. The plants will do the growing (learning) themselves. They grow naturally. The teacher's role includes: finding the right soil and nutrients; perhaps putting them in the right spot; generally leaving them to themselves but paying close attention to their progress and stepping in to help when needed. Of course, pruning may be needed from time to time. Contrast this with a 'website to surfers' where you see yourself as a resource to be used as and when your learners see fit.

The following are examples of metaphors that capture how you may relate to your learners:

- law enforcer to the potentially criminal;
- carer to the vulnerable;
- salesperson to potential buyer;
- sheepdog to sheep;
- sherpa to mountaineer;
- explorer to fellow explorers;

- beekeeper to beehive;
- conductor to orchestra;
- guide to tourists on a tour bus.

Task 6

Explore your current conception of the roles of teacher and learner by asking:

- What is your theory of teaching? (Ramsden)
- At what level do you operate? (Biggs and Tang)
- If you have completed the Teaching Perspectives Inventory, what do you score highly on, including the sub-scores of belief, intention, and action?
- Which metaphor comes closest to how you relate to learners?

2   Participation

Question 13: An hour lecture is a very small duration. Does active learning (i.e. taking time out for activities) detract from the practical imperative of delivering the lecture?

The wording of this question is revealing because it refers to 'active learning' and 'delivering a lecture'. The former refers to learners' activity, the latter to lecturer activity. There is an old cartoon depicted in three panels. The first shows a boy with his dog and his friend. The boy says, 'I taught Spot to whistle'. In the second, the friend looks expectantly at the silent dog and says, 'I don't hear him whistling'. In the final panel, the boy says, 'I said I taught him. I didn't say he learnt anything'.

The beginnings of an answer to this question can be found in Donald Bligh's account of the diagram shown in Figure 4. A group of learners was given an hour's lecture. Some members of the group (Group A) were given a short test at the end of the lecture. This showed they retained on average about 50 percent of the content of the lecture. When tested again after a week they retained just a little less; when tested again after 63 days they still retained most of that.

Group B were not given the test at the end of the lecture but rather a day later. They retained about 30 percent of the material and when tested fourteen days later they still retained most of that. The remainder of the diagram shows the retention of Goups C, D, and E, each of whose initial testing was later. The most significant aspect of this diagram for me is that Group A retained more after nine weeks than Group B did after one day (Bligh 1998: 46–47). This suggests that if you want learners to remember the content of a lecture, they need to re-engage with that content, to rehearse it, *before they leave the room*.

In this instance, the rehearsal took the form of a test at the end of an hour. It need not be a test and you do not have to wait until the end of an hour. Rather, you could plan for, say, twenty minutes of information giving, after

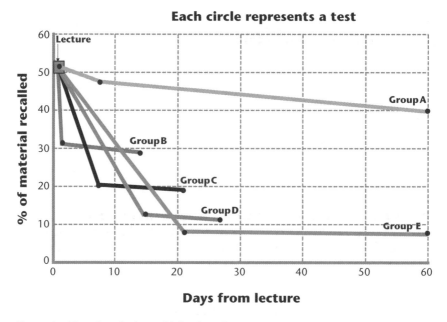

Figure 4. The value of rehearsal following a lecture.

which the learners carry out an activity that requires them to engage with that information. Activities such as those listed in Questions 6 and 7 could be used for this. This enables learners to be active and to work with the information you have supplied. In this way, they will be able not just to remember the information, but also to become practised in what it is you want them to be able to do with the information – to critique it, compare it, apply it, plan to use it, and so on. This activity on their part can then be followed by a further chunk of information from you.

The most common objection of the lecturer to this idea goes like this: 'I'm obliged to cover a certain amount of material and if I include learners' activities in my time with them, I won't be able to cover everything'. The crucial question in response to this is, '*You* are covering the material. What are the *learners* covering?'

Phil Race reports on the range of activities that learners really engage in during lectures. I have drawn from and added to his list:

- copying things down without thinking about them;
- gazing out of the window (not necessarily a sign of inattention – see Question 44);

- looking at other learners;
- worrying;
- watching the clock;
- doodling;
- daydreaming;
- sleeping;
- reading something that has nothing to do with the lecture;
- watching something that has nothing to do with the lecture;
- writing something that has nothing to do with the lecture;
- listening to a MP3 player;
- feeling unwell;
- exchanging texts.

(adapted from Race 2006: 98)

It is possible for learners to be present in body but not in mind. Just because you are covering the material and talking to them, it does not mean they are learning.

You may feel a compulsion to say or show key knowledge or may even be under direction to do so. However, unless the learners are encouraged or indeed forced to engage with it, they are unlikely to hear everything you say. So, while active learning may detract from the delivery of the lecture, perhaps that is no great loss. The truth is that although you are fulfilling your obligation by saying to the learners everything they need to hear, they are probably not hearing all of it, still less understanding it or knowing how to use it.

Even if all you want them to do is to receive information – if the objectives for the session are at the lower end of Bloom's taxonomy – talking at them could be one of the less effective ways for the information to be received. The use of online material, podcasts, and video lectures means that the learners can access the information at a time and place to suit them, rewinding when they need to hear something again, breaking the lecture down into 'bite-size' chunks if they wish; pausing and making a note; pausing to discuss with others, and so on.

If information can be received other than through the lecture, it is worth asking, 'what can you as a teacher bring to the delivery that makes it worthwhile?' The teacher can provide:

- an opportunity for questions to be asked and answered;
- alternative explanations of difficult ideas;
- personal qualities that can inspire the learner – enthusiasm, passion, commitment, humour;
- storytelling powers – off-the-cuff illustrations, anecdotes, and examples;
- questioning skills.

In the same way, the group of learners is a great 'resource' for learning. If learning is helped by interaction, discussion, and dialogue, the learners themselves are perhaps the most valuable resource when they are gathered together, more so than the expert and their materials. 'Facilitator' is a much-abused term but it does describe the potential role of the teacher when attempting to make the most of this gathering of learners by orchestrating focused, structured interactions between those present.

Ultimately, this leads you to question what is the best use of the time when you find yourself in a room with a group of learners. One option is for you, as an expert, to say things at them – but that is just one.

Question 14: Can you use film clips as your rest period, which then flows into the next part of the learning? The analysis comes after the watching. Does this count as a rest?

A related question was,

> 'In a recent lecture I punctuated my presentation with mini presentations given by a colleague. This was done in a structured and planned way. What are the benefits and disadvantages of using this method?'

The point about having a 'rest' is indeed to give the learners a rest from having to listen to you. In that sense, to have to look at a film clip is a rest. But the principle behind the rest goes a little deeper. It is about what the learner is expected to do. If they switch from listening to you to watching and listening to a clip, you are still expecting broadly the same behaviour from them – that is, sitting, silent, listening, perhaps taking notes. You are varying the ways in which you direct them to be passive. The same applies if you and your colleague alternate presentations. The real break they need is from that behaviour, so it will be more effective to ask them to be doing something different such as planning, analysing, questioning each other, and so on. Your question should not be 'How can I hold their attention?' but 'To which task should I direct their attention?'

If you want your learners to be passive and hopefully attentive, it can help to have variety in what you want them to pay attention to – you, slides, a DVD or (with smaller groups) flipchart/whiteboard. The use of relevant pictures, diagrams, and other visuals will assist learners' learning. Exley and Dennick suggest four advantages that result from their use:

- they can enhance understanding of a complicated idea or process;
- they can grab and keep attention;

- they aid memory – it is far easier for a student to remember a visual explanation than a series of words;
- they can be entertaining and help create a relaxed and positive atmosphere

(Exley and Dennick 2009: 87)

A linked question was as follows:

'Does talking imply active learning? Active learning might equally be achieved by activities that promote different types of listening'.

This links to what you might do when showing a DVD – you could provide some guidance for how to watch it. Here are three examples:

1. Say 'Please write down verbatim anything you see or hear that you find challenging, significant, puzzling, to prepare for the activity that follows'. The activity that follows is where you ask them perhaps in pairs or threes to agree on, say, the three most important things for them in the DVD and compare notes with another group or report back briefly to the whole group.
2. You can simply provide a handout with a set of headings that describe the main parts of the clip, each followed by a blank space for notes.
3. You can divide up the task:

   - Group A take note of x (aspect of the clip)
   - Group B take note of y (another aspect of the clip)
   - Group C take note of z (another aspect of the clip)

   Afterwards arrange for groups of three, each comprising a member of group A, a member of group B, and a member of group C, to compare and integrate notes.

Another question asked was:

'Is a break at the twenty-minute point absolutely necessary if the lecture itself is by design constantly peppered with small breaks for question-and-answer sessions throughout?'

Ask yourself, what was the behaviour of the majority of members of the group during the question-and-answer sessions? Most often, your answer will reflect that question-and-answer sessions do not involve everyone. For those who don't participate, they are a break from listening exclusively to you but not from being passive.

Question 15: How can you get *all* students to actively engage?

I was observing a lecture once with around seventy learners and the lecturer asked the learners to form buzz groups. She provided them with a specific task to do in groups of two or three, for just three minutes. Although the majority of learners appeared to be working on the task, one of a pair of learners near to me took this as a cue to read the newspaper and the other to file her nails. They did not take the request seriously. You may need to recognize that in a large group it is possible that a portion of learners will not engage in a short, small group task and they may instead text, talk about last night, talk about tonight, and so on. In a sense, this is no worse than if you had carried on talking. They may not have been 'present' while you were talking either. (See the list of what learners do in lectures in Question 13.) It is just that when you ask for a task to be done, their disengagement becomes more evident. So one response to this question is simply to recognize and accept that you can't be sure to engage all of the learners all of the time in small group work. This should not stop you going around and encouraging the non-participants if you wish.

There are many reasons why some learners do not engage in small group work and you can take steps to prevent these in the way in which the task is set up. Learners are more likely to engage when:

- *The task is clear.* Too often, teachers ask small groups to 'discuss your response' or they ask an ambiguous or overcomplicated question. Keep it simple, explain it once or at the most twice.
- *The task is achievable*, given the understanding of the group and the time available.
- *A clear outcome is required.* For example, 'agree as a group on the three steps you would take/the two questions you would ask/four ways to tackle the problem/come up with a definition of', and so on.
- *The time for the task is fixed.*
- *The group is of the right size.* In a group of six or more, it is more likely that one or more group members will not get the chance to speak and it may be harder for agreement to be reached. Stick to pairs, threes, fours or fives and be prescriptive about this.

There are other things to take heed of, which might provide an answer to another question asked:

'How do you engage a large group of learners (70) (Masters level) into an interactive session when they hate any group work exercise?'

(A collective groan goes around the room when I say 'in your groups')

To avoid the groan, consider the following:

- Determine the composition of the groups (see Question 34).
- Avoid the 'let's hear feedback from every group on a flipchart' technique (see Question 41).
- You have to believe in what you are doing. If group work doesn't inspire you or you are doing it because you can't think of any alternative, it's unlikely to engage the learners.
- Provide an explanation for why you are asking them to work in groups, preferably with an illustration of the difference it made to previous learners.
- If there is flexibility with the room layout, arrange it so that it is easy for learners to work in groups.

Another question asked was:

'When I want the learners to do group work they are sometimes reluctant to move the furniture, they want to have discussions, etc., while sitting in rows. How can I make them hop up enthusiastically and move to a circle?'

First, consider arranging the furniture before the session if that is possible or getting the learners to help you do this at the start. Second, a circle can be useful if you want everyone to clearly see each other for a group discussion. It can also be very intimidating for some learners and make them less likely to contribute. A room arrangement that has learners seated in small groups but also able to see you and the rest of the group is likely to work.

But, be patient – often lecturers tell me that the first time they tried group work or a new activity, they were anxious and on the verge of giving up but they persevered and were eventually successful.

If your concern is

'How to bring out the quiet learners to contribute more without causing them fear and panic?',

then consider using techniques such as 'pyramids' or 'five minutes each way' as outlined in Question 7 – the kinds of activity from which it is impossible to escape without talking to at least one person but where you do not have to talk in front of the whole group.

Question 16: Should different teaching methods be discussed with students?

This echoes the point in the last question about explaining why you are using group work. The least you should do in this respect, when meeting a group for the first time (or even the only time), is to let the learners know how you intend to teach and what you expect them to do as learners. Anyone who is a learner has expectations of what that involves. These expectations are often based on their previous experiences of being a learner. When you have a new group, of course, the learners in that group will bring with them a range of expectations that may differ wildly. Some will expect to be silent and passive, some will expect that they will be asked their opinion, some will expect that they are responsible for helping their peers learn, some will expect they can challenge what the teacher says. Each of these expectations will have a complementary expectation of what the teacher should be doing.

If you let your learners know right from the start what methods you are going to use, then even if they do not welcome those methods, they will know what to expect and can prepare for it. Alternatively, if the group is of a suitable size, you can listen to what their expectations are before explaining the approach you are going to take. You may even think it is appropriate to negotiate the methods used. One way to find out expectations is to take the list from Question 53, 'As a student I expect', distribute it or your adaptation of it, ask learners to complete it, check on their responses, and indicate the extent to which your intentions match their expectations.

If you do see a group regularly and they come to realize that your approach to teaching methods is always guided by what you think will be most useful for them, then eventually you will be in a position to try out new methods with them and to tell them you are doing so. If they know you have their best interests at heart, they are more likely to trust in you and be ready to go with your experiment.

The metaphors exercise was introduced in Question 12 to encourage you to think about your conception of what teaching is and therefore what learning is. Perhaps you could use those ideas with your learners to find out their preferred metaphor. How would they like to be treated? How would they like to use you as a teacher?

Question 17: How influential should the size of the student group be on your style of teaching?

A linked question was:

'How would you include an interactive element with a large group of 100+?'

Most of the activities for active and interactive learning described in Questions 6 and 7 can be used with groups of any size. The only two that would obviously be unsuitable would be rounds and fishbowls.

Of course, with a larger group, you may feel less confident about introducing activities. The logistics of getting into groups of two or three, the noise created by so many people talking, the prospect of failing to bring everyone back to attention or the likelihood that a number of the audience will not join in can deter you. However, never forget just how numbing the alternative experience of sitting listening to you for an hour can be!

The following are additional pointers for small group activities within a large group:

- Ensure the instructions are on a slide or otherwise clearly visible to everyone.
- Make sure you have a plan for how to regain attention, such as using a countdown clock with sound effects on your screen or simply by clapping your hands.
- Remember it is generally best to keep the activities short.
- Recognize the limitations on getting feedback from the group afterwards.

Question 18: What techniques do you suggest for generating questions from students?

Simply asking 'Any questions?' often fails to get a response or gets questions from just a small minority of the audience. This is understandable because some learners fear speaking in a large group or asking a question that might be seen by others as obvious or off the point. Here are some ways of getting learners to at least phrase a question and possibly to ask it.

Ask everyone to write down a question (about the topic in general or what has been covered so far) on a scrap of paper. Have the papers passed down to the front. Ensure you have time during an activity to look through these questions and select the ones that it would be most useful to address. Take the time to respond to some of the questions. No-one need be identified as the questioner unless they choose to be. The attention of the group is usually greater for this than if you had simply supplied the same information unprompted. Even those learners whose questions have not been read out will have to engage simply by wording a question.

I heard of a lecturer who tried this technique and, exasperated that nobody had asked the most important question, picked up one scrap of paper and read out the question he wished someone had asked, rather than what was on the scrap of paper. The learners did not realize he had done this!

A variation on this exercise, for a large group, is to ask the learners to write down a question as above. Then ask them to swap it, swap again, and maybe again, until each person is holding a question that was not written by them or by the individuals on either side of them. You can then point to or name an individual and ask them to read out the question they have. They will do this knowing that if the question is 'stupid' it will not reflect on them. If you supplied Post-its® for writing the questions on, these could be displayed later.

You can ask learners to come up with a question in pairs or small groups using strategies such as the following:

> 'Now that you have heard X's theory, imagine we could bring X into this lecture theatre now. What is the one question you would like to ask X if X were here?'

> 'Imagine you are the prosecution putting together a case against X's ideas in court. What question would you ask that might put X on the spot?'

Question 19: What do you do as the lecturer while the group is engaged in an activity? I feel a bit self-conscious standing around at the front

The time when the learners are engaged in an activity provides you with a valuable opportunity to review, prepare, and observe.

- *Review*: reassess what you have just said and how the learners reacted. Do you need to revisit any part of the last section, perhaps to add to an explanation, give a better response to a question, clarify a point that you made?
- *Prepare*: remind yourself of what you will be saying and doing next. If appropriate, are the materials ready for distribution, is the slide ready to show?
- *Observe*: watch the learners as they are engaged in the activity. In particular, check the body language. Are any individuals less engaged than you would expect, can you tell if the groups are tackling the assigned task, or discussing something else or are turned off. Are they going to finish on time, early or late? Do you need to go round to check on progress?

If the activity is an engaging one, it is most likely that the group will not notice what you are doing.

Question 20: In a seminar context, is it more effective for students to learn from their peers through discussion or team work (possibly omitting aspects they don't know) or to impart clear structured knowledge?

There are substantial benefits to be derived from peer learning, which David Boud defines as 'students learning from and with each other in both formal and informal ways' (Boud 2001: 4). He suggests five outcomes from peer learning.

1. *Working with others*. Peer learning can provide practice in planning and teamwork and develop in the learner a sense of responsibility for their own and others' learning. Increased confidence and self-esteem can result from engaging in a community of learning and learners.

2. *Critical enquiry and reflection*. Boud cites studies that show that critical reflection and reassessment of views is more likely to come from interchange between peers than from discussion sessions with teachers. 'Students are often better able to reflect on and explore ideas when the presence and authority of a staff member do not influence them'.

3. *Communication and articulation of knowledge, understanding, and skills*. Often, it is only when a student has the opportunity to express their understanding and perhaps have it challenged that they can develop a sense of how substantial their understanding is. There are few opportunities for this outside of peer learning.

4. *Managing learning and how to learn*. Peer learning demands skills in managing yourself and others to ensure an effective learning experience. Some forms of peer learning involve 'a group of students taking collective responsibility for identifying their own learning needs and planning how these might be addressed'. This is a process that should stand students in good stead in many areas outside of formal studies.

5. *Self and peer assessment*. Peer learning provides a student with a context for receiving feedback on their work and giving feedback on the work of others. It has been suggested that feedback is the most powerful influence on students' achievements at university and it is rarely the case that tutors have time to give sufficient feedback to all students. This process also makes the student more proficient in self-assessment, an essential life skill.

(adapted from Boud 2001: 8–9)

Boud notes that peer learning 'can be described as a way of moving beyond independent to *interdependent* or mutual learning' (ibid.: 3).

Arranging for your learners to experience the benefits of peer learning in a seminar does not exclude you from also imparting knowledge and checking on learning. Two key questions in preparing for peer learning are:

1. How much preparation, even training, do the learners need to play their role?
2. How directive should you be? You want them to take responsibility but not be left floundering. If you want to encourage learners to work independently, it is important for you to be very explicit and detailed about the process that you want them to follow.

Question 20 asks about the particular context of a seminar but there are many strategies for using peer learning during a course. Other examples include:

- action learning sets (see Question 34);
- patchwork text assessment (see Question 49);
- (for teachers as learners) peer observation of teaching (see Question 54).

Remember that peer learning is not confined to group work – it can also be one-to-one.

The following is an example of a structured group activity that involves peer learning and that might be suitable for a seminar. The method is known as a crossover or sometimes a jigsaw.

Assume a group of 30. Divide the learners up into six groups of five. Each group of five is given a different case study in written form, for example a case study. The task is in two stages.

For the first stage, each group has to read their case study, discuss it and consult the teacher if necessary to ensure they all have a common understanding of the content. They then have to prepare a summary and analysis of the case study. In the second stage, five new groups are formed. Each group will have six members – one from each of the original six groups. When they are assembled in their new groups, each member takes their turn in presenting the summary and analysis they acquired in their first group. Of course, there is time for discussion and questions in the groups in this second stage.

When this works well, the learner has had to read, discuss, teach, and listen en route to learning about six case studies.

Don't have more than six members in a group. If you are confident and thoroughly prepared, you can operate this activity with larger groups, such as sixty learners divided into two parallel crossovers – that is, two sets of six by five. If the numbers don't divide neatly, arrange that some learners will retain a partner from their first group when moving to the second.

Question 21: What's the best way to obtain feedback as to how things are going and whether learners are happy?

I am not sure there are reliable strategies for revealing to what extent your learners are 'happy' but it is certainly possible to check on their learning. It is common when lecturing to a large group for lecturers to feel out of touch with their audience. It can be very difficult to tell whether your lectures are working well or not. You need to adopt deliberate strategies if you want to find out how you are doing. Suggested strategies include:

- keypads
- instant questionnaires
- three most important things
- minute papers
- the muddiest point

Keypads

Many institutions now have keypad equipment, also known as electronic voting systems (EVS), which is an excellent means for getting feedback on your learners' understanding during or at the end of a session. A popular use of the keypad that many people are familiar with is in the 'Ask the Audience' slot of the TV programme, 'Who Wants to be a Millionaire?'

Each learner or group of two or three learners has a keypad – normally a handheld device, although there some are built into the backs of seats in lecture theatres. Software is loaded into your computer. You display a question on the screen that invites a response by pressing the appropriate key on the remote – A, B, C, D, etc.

After a fixed amount of time, say sixty seconds, all responses from the group are displayed on the screen as a bar chart or pie chart or in whatever form you have requested. This provides you with an instant picture of what the group as a whole thinks or has understood. Learners find the equipment easy to use and appreciate that the responses are anonymous. If you use this to establish the degree of understanding of your learners, the findings may indicate that you need to revisit a particular point or explanation.

Following the introduction of keypads in lectures, lecturers from Kingston University found that learners 'became more receptive learners, their experiences of social alienation in the large lecture diminished as they became active in their small groups, and they appeared to behave in a more empowered way' (Mazikunas et al. 2009: 210).

In the absence of keypads, you can still get a quick response from the group about their understanding as follows: Each learner is given, say, four pieces of paper, each of a different colour. These could be integrated into the module guide as A4 card dividers. The colours provide a substitute for the keypad letters – 'Display blue if you think A is the answer, red if you think B', and so on. They hold up the corresponding piece of paper to show their answer. This gives the teacher an approximate picture of the group's understanding.

Instant questionnaires

Another strategy is to use instant questionnaires. All you have to do is to display a rating scale on a slide or (with a smaller group) on a flipchart. For example:

A = Always true for me
B = Often true for me
C = Sometimes true for me
D = Seldom true for me
E = Never true for me

You then read out a series of statements, which are your best guesses about what is going on for the learners in your lectures. For example:

1. I understand the lecture content.
2. I have encountered this material before.
3. My lecture notes are incomplete and probably inaccurate.
4. The pace is a bit slow.
5. I have questions that I need answers to.
6. Paying attention all through a lecture is a real struggle.

Learners take a piece of their own paper and write down the numbers of the six statements. Against each they simply write the letter that indicates to what extent the statement is true for them, as follows:

1. B
2. B
3. C
4. A
5. D
6. B

You then simply ask the learners to leave their pieces of paper in a tray as they leave and collate the data to see if your hunches are borne out. With very large classes you would not need to ask all learners. A sample consisting of the front and back rows, and two rows in the middle, would be sufficient.

Of course, you can devise an instant questionnaire while the session is in progress and make it specific to that session. For instance, you could use the following ratings scale:

A = Strongly agree
B = Agree
C = Don't know or unsure
D = Disagree
E = Strongly disagree

with these questions:

1. This lecture contained too much information.
2. In a room as overcrowded as this we need a break half-way through.
3. I'd like to spend more time on x in the next lecture.
4. I could use all four techniques introduced today.
5. I could explain y's theory to a friend.
6. I would like more examples of z.

It is such a quick and uncomplicated device that it is possible to use it regularly to check on progress or concerns, and to determine whether steps you have taken in response to previous instant questionnaire feedback have had the desired effect.

Three most important things

Listing the 'three most important things' at the end of your lecture can be used as a means of summarizing the lecture at its close to highlight its most important features. This same device can be used to check what the group has learnt. You could say:

> 'I'd like to check whether I've got my main points across. I'd like you all to write down the three most important things about this lecture: those three things that, if you forgot everything else, would capture the essence of the lecture for you. You have two minutes'.

While the learners are doing this you write down what you think are the three most important things on a slide. When the two minutes are up you display your slide and briefly explain your three points and why they are the most important. You then ask for a show of hands.

'Who, honestly, has written down all three of these points? Who has written down two? Who one? Who none? What other points did people consider important?'

If this seems too threatening to learners, you can do any of the following:

- emphasize that what is on trial is your own competence as a teacher rather than their competence as learners;
- ask for their points before revealing your own;
- collect learners' written statements to read in private;
- emphasize the scope that exists for alternative perspectives, different conclusions, etc.

This exercise can be very salutary.

Minute papers

Thomas Angelo and Patricia Cross (1993) suggest a number of strategies for finding out how you are doing in *Classroom Assessment Techniques*, including minute papers.

Just before the end of the class, ask learners to write a response in one or two sentences to the following questions:

- What was the most important thing you learned during this session?
- What important question remains unanswered as we end this session?

Collect these responses in.

The 'muddiest' point

At the end of a lecture, ask each learner to write down on a scrap of paper what, for them, was the 'muddiest' point in this session; in other words, what was *least* clear to them. Collect these in. Look through them. Start the next session with the group by going over what were the most frequent muddiest points: 'I am just going to go over the two/three areas that you had most trouble with last time'.

This technique was developed by Frederick Mosteller, a professor of statistics at Harvard University. For a detailed account of its development and use, see Mosteller (1989), which is also available at: http://isites.harvard.edu/fs/html/icb. topic58474/mosteller.html

3   Performance

Question 22: How do you keep the attention of a large group of students?

The advice given in Question 14 is to put energy into planning where to *direct* their attention, and not to attempt to *hold* it for long periods of time. When you *do* seek to keep their attention, here are eight things to consider.

- making an emotional connection
- enthusiasm
- use of stories
- non-intrusive materials
- your non-verbal communication
- pausing
- humour
- simplicity

Making an emotional connection. It has been suggested that a great talk is a series of emotional moments for the audience. There is a brief discussion in Question 4 about how to get attention in the initial few minutes of a lecture. The same principles apply throughout your time with the group. When people recall great lectures, they associate them with the feelings they provoked, such as inspired, intrigued, motivated, fascinated, amused, astounded, thrilled or enlightened. The best speakers are aware of this, often intuitively or unconsciously, so when planning it is worth asking yourself how you want the audience to feel at different points in your talk. If you are clear about this to yourself, it can significantly affect your planning, as it can influence your content and the sequence and manner in which you deliver it. You will be recognizing that the cognitive coherence of your talk will almost certainly not be enough to hook the audience. You are simultaneously the playwright, whose lines will grab the audience's attention, and the actor, who has not only to remember the lines but deliver them to maximum effect.

Enthusiasm. Most teachers are naturally enthusiastic about what they teach, as it is bound up with their interest and research and experience. However, the enthusiasm you need is not just for the subject but enthusiasm about being there and helping others learn about it. A new lecturer was looking back on her experience as a learner in higher education and recalled her 'best' lecturer. When asked what made him so special, she said, 'He so obviously wanted to be there and his enthusiasm for being with the class was infectious'.

Use of stories. The use of stories is pivotal in gaining, retaining or indeed regaining attention. Stories can be scripted or improvised, short or lengthy, true or fictional, about you or about others. If you use one to illustrate a point, you can be sure that the story will be more likely to lodge in the listener's mind more than any set of bullet points from a PowerPoint slide. Stories stick.

While gaining attention, stories can also aid learning in several ways:

1. By stimulating simultaneous conscious and unconscious learning.
2. If you deliberately announce that you are going to tell a story and if it is a lengthy one, encourage the audience to 'sit back while I tell this story'. In doing so, you will encourage a state of mind where learners put less energy into 'trying' to learn and give more space to unconscious learning (see Question 50).
3. By making an emotional connection.
4. By making abstract ideas concrete.
5. By helping learners to assimilate – that is, making links between new and existing knowledge.
6. By helping learners to 'structurize'. Margeret Parkin reports on work by Roberta and Gerald Evans who found that undergraduates taught with metaphors, stories, and analogies demonstrated fewer conceptual and technical errors than those taught without. Also, those taught with stories were better at applying the concepts of what they had learnt to more far-reaching and novel situations, which is described as 'stucturizing' (Parkin 1998: 16–17).
7. By changing the dynamic in the classroom.

Purposes for which stories can be used include:

- to introduce or wrap up a session;
- to illustrate a teaching point;
- as case studies/discussion starters;

- to teach facts and sequences;
- to amuse;
- to help the listeners to deal with something novel.

Questions to ask in preparing to use a story as part of your session include:

- What's the purpose?
- Will you read it or tell it in your own words?
- How will you introduce it?
- Have you remembered that the power is not in your performance but in the processes that the story stimulates and in your authenticity and naturalness in telling it?
- How long will it last?
- Do you need to reveal/explain the meaning?
- Will you use one story or many?
- Does the story have the potential to arouse strong emotions in the listeners and, if so, are you ready to deal with this?

Non-intrusive materials. As noted in Question 4, you might want deliberately not to show a slide when introducing or finishing the session. Although this is the conventional thing to do, consider where you want learners to focus their attention and, if you want them to connect with you, make sure that you are where the attention should be exclusively focused at the start of the session. Then you may use slides if that is what you need to do. Also remember the value of using button 'B' on the keyboard to give a black screen or button 'W' to give a white screen during a slide show.

Similar principles apply to handouts. Have you ever done or witnessed this? The lecturer distributes the handout and the learners quite naturally start to look through the handout and then the lecturer feels exasperated that not everyone is paying attention when they start to talk.

Your non-verbal communication. This has more of an effect than you probably believe. However carefully you have prepared your talk and materials, recognize that aspects of your non-verbal communication may override the content of your session. If you do not already know the answer to the questions that follow, find out and check to see if your non-verbal communication is likely to enhance or to impede your message.

- What do you sound like? Do you vary your pitch and tone?
- What are your facial expressions?
- What is your posture?
- Do you move around and, if so, in what way and how much do you move around?

- Do you have any traits – fiddling with a ring on your finger, clicking a pen, hands in pockets, adjusting glasses? Most lecturers can recall from their time as learners a lecturer who had a particularly annoying or comical habit that was the main focus of learners' attention in lectures, rather than the content.

Consider getting a video recording of yourself teaching. Just about everyone I have met who has seen a recording of themselves teaching says two things: 'It was awful' and 'It was really useful'.

Pausing. Stopping talking from time to time can increase the audience's attention. It:

- helps you manage the pace;
- gives you time to think;
- shows control;
- enhances command;
- marks a divide in a lecture and prepares for a fresh start.

Humour. See Question 24

Simplicity. Simplicity can help attention. Not simplifying complex ideas but making the outline clear and minimal. Ask as you prepare to talk, 'what's the simplest way of conveying the content, without simplifying it?'

Task 7

Visit www.ted.com. Here you can find a collection of talks, none of which is supposed to last more than eighteen minutes, by experts in different fields from around the world. Look to see if you can spot any of the above techniques or indeed others.

Question 23: What could I do to communicate better?

The most important sets of communication skills for teachers are:

- explaining
- listening
- asking questions (see Question 29)
- responding to learners' questions and comments (see Question 29)

Explaining is the one thing you will almost certainly have to do as a teacher, whatever your subject, whether you are talking to one or to two hundred. Here are some ideas on how to give an effective explanation:

1. Beforehand, check on the amount of information you want to give – remember the constraints of time and the likely receptivity of the learners.
2. Beforehand, decide on the key points.
3. Make sure you understand what you are talking about. This may sound initially absurd but many lecturers testify that they only really understood a topic when they had to teach it for the first time. The knowledge of the topic that sufficed when you wrote an essay on it or passed an exam in it, or even carried out research, can be different from that knowledge which enables you to dismantle it, reassemble it, and present it to others. In particular, imagine the most awkward question that might be asked and how you would deal with it. This is even more important with an unfamiliar topic (see Question 48).
4. Check what your learners already know about the topic. If you don't, you may be assuming knowledge they don't have, which will make your explanation harder to follow, or ignoring knowledge they already have, and thus needlessly repeating it. Of course, this means that you need to be ready to modify your explanation if the learners' existing knowledge is less or more than you expected. There is guidance on how to find out about learners' existing knowledge in Question 31.
5. Provide a clear introduction and framework.
6. Make sure you define new words or terms that you use. It is very easy to use terms or acronyms that you are familiar with and to forget that they may not be known to all of the audience. Most learners will be reluctant to interrupt to ask for clarification. Just include a brief definition the first time that you use the term.
7. Pause from time to time. Teachers are notorious for talking at length. A pause will give learners time to review what you have just said and perhaps to ask a question.
8. Make sure there is opportunity for questions. Your pauses may lead to questions. If not, don't forget to invite them.
9. Check your learners' understanding. There are some examples in Question 21 on how to do this. You could also pose a multiple-choice question and get feedback from a show of hands.
10. Go at a pace that suits the learner(s). This implies that you will be ready to change your explanation in light of checking their understanding.
11. Relate the explanation to their experience. We learn by making connections to what we already know. New information builds on or challenges existing knowledge. The good learner will make these

connections readily. You can help by giving examples of how the new
information relates to what they already (probably) know.

12. Give examples.
13. Go from the concrete to the abstract. The convention is to provide the
    theory and then illustrate with examples but the brain can find it
    easier to grasp an abstraction if it has first been presented with a con-
    crete example.
14. Use visual aids if appropriate. This could be a drawing, a picture, a
    diagram or an object. Some of your learners will prefer the visual to
    the linguistic.
15. Help the learners visualize your explanation by your descriptions or
    by your use of hand movements.
16. Use anecdotes if you know any. The points made in Question 22 about
    the power of stories relate to this. Any impromptu or planned tale that
    illustrates the point will be likely to be remembered.
17. Use analogies.
18. Repeat key points, perhaps rephrasing them. If it is a key point, it needs
    repeating. Sometimes, the listener will understand second time around
    or have the initial learning reinforced if the point is reworded.
19. Be clear where one part ends and another begins and what the link is
    between them.
20. Summarize as you go on.
21. Summarize at the end.

Task 8

Review an explanation you have given recently. How many of the 21 items above
do you recall using?

Teachers are often far better explainers than they are listeners. The common conception of the teacher's role is as a transmitter of knowledge and there
are certainly many opportunities to practise the skills of explaining. Listening,
or rather active listening, is much less commonly perceived to be central to the
teacher's role. The skills of active listening are normally thought to apply when
one person is listening to another and wishes to encourage that person to talk
and explore at length a particular problem, task or concern that preoccupies
them. This is useful, for instance, in being a personal tutor. Being an effective
active listener means being able to draw on a repertoire of listening skills and
knowing which of them is appropriate at any given moment when listening to
another.

When teaching a group, these skills would still generally be directed at one person. In particular, the skills from the list below of paraphrasing, asking open questions, clarifying, summarizing, and even managing silence can be used to help an individual articulate their own thoughts and answers. In using these skills, the teacher is literally the facilitator of another's learning. They are not in the role where they supply answers and simply tell. These skills are especially important in small group teaching, when the teacher wants to generate discussion among the group.

The following are some of the skills of active listening:

- *Non-verbal*: conveying that you are attentive and that you have understood through communicating other than with words, including your posture, eye contact, tone of voice, facial expression.
- *Listening*: paying attention to what is being said and suppressing your impatience, desire to be in control or any other form of 'mental buzz' that is interfering with you paying attention.
- *Reflecting feelings*: telling the speaker what feelings they are communicating to you, what the speaker may have articulated or that may be evident from what they have said and how they have said it (e.g. 'it sounds as though you were surprised'; 'I guess you were relieved').
- *Paraphrasing*: telling the speaker what they have just said – sometimes verbatim, sometimes using different words but retaining the meaning. This confirms that you have heard, not passed judgement, and are inviting the speaker to continue, which they normally do.
- *Use of questions*: posing questions, especially open questions (beginning with 'how' or 'what'), with the intention of helping the speaker to clarify their thoughts and explore their ideas more fully.
- *Summarizing*: drawing together what the speaker has said and presenting it back to them.
- *Clarifying*: checking your understanding of what the speaker is saying to you.
- *Challenging/confronting*: helping the speaker to be more aware of what they are saying, by gently drawing their attention to inconsistencies and discrepancies in their statements.
- *Managing silence*: when the speaker stops speaking, not taking that as a cue for you to start speaking, but remaining fully attentive.

Question 24: Do you have any advice on using humour in a lecture?

Humour can help learning. Eric Jensen suggests that the changes in the chemical balance of the blood brought about by laughter may boost the production of the neurotransmitters needed for alertness and memory (Jensen 1995: 35).

Lecturers often assume that humour is inappropriate, given the formality of the situation and their role as 'leader' of the session. If you are naturally humorous in everyday exchanges, it is OK to bring that into your teaching. If you are not naturally humorous, don't even think about it. Also remember that humour is in a sense a tool to aid learning and don't take the route of a lecturer I knew, where the humour becomes the end rather than a means, leaving the learners entertained but not educated. On the other hand, you don't have to be so rigid as the lecturer I heard of who set out to tell a joke punctually every twenty minutes.

Ronald Berk (2003) extols the virtues of humour and suggests how to use it in *Professors are from Mars, Students are from Snickers*. Kevin McCarron is both a lecturer and a stand-up comedian. He has written with Maggi Savin-Baden on how some of the techniques practised by stand-up comedians can inform teaching in higher education. However, their focus is not on humour but on techniques that 'provoke, irritate, bemuse, confuse and even anger their audience' (McCarron and Savin-Baden 2008: 356); in other words, challenge learners in order to help their learning.

Question 25: How do you combat/overcome lecturing nerves?

This is the most commonly asked question by far of all fifty-five in this book. Other variations on it are:

> 'How do I cope with nervousness? I tend to talk fast when under pressure!'

> 'How do I stop my voice fluctuating from high to low pitch compatible with how fast my heart is beating?'

> 'How to be cool, calm, and collected in front of eighty-three learners?'

> 'Do you have any tips for reducing nerves or inspiring confidence, particularly for the start of a session?'

> 'How can I calm my nerves before AND during the session?'

Here are some things you can do.

- Try breathing exercises to slow your pulse rate. For instance, breathe in deeply, counting slowly to five, then breathe out to the count of seven. You may need to do this before you start or during the session.

- Make sure you have a drink of water to hand during the session to prevent you experiencing a dry throat.
- Make sure that you are not holding notes or any other paper or object while talking, which will show the learners that you are shaking.
- If it is possible, get to the room before anyone arrives. This gives you time to arrange any furniture or materials. Most importantly, however, you can establish where you are going to stand and what your view will be – you may even want to take a few moments in that spot and begin to 'command the room'.
- If you are there as people begin to enter the room, talking with individuals as the room fills can be relaxing for you and help you feel less separate before you start.
- Being fully prepared helps enormously. Many people become more relaxed when they have paid attention to every detail in advance – of what they are going to say, of when and how they will be using materials such as slides or handouts. In particular, if you are able to learn exactly what you are going to say in the first five minutes or so, this can help because by the time you have got through those five minutes you will be 'into' the session and will not be so nervous.
- Consider arranging for the learners to do a very brief activity, say two or three minutes, very early on in the session. When they do this, it changes the mood in the room, it gives you a break from talking, and it gives you the chance to take stock and remind yourself of what you are going to do and say next.
- Perhaps the most potent strategy for countering nerves is to attend to what I would call the mindset with which you approach the session. Many new lecturers say that as they approach initial sessions, they often see themselves as being 'on trial'. They are waiting to be found out as not knowing as much as their learners think they do. There is a powerful chain of cause and effect in operation here. The way you perceive the situation – that is, your mindset – affects how you feel; the way you feel affects the way you behave; the way you behave affects the way the learners respond.

Imagine the sequence for the mindset of 'on trial': Feeling anxious and nervous leads to hesitant behaviour, which leads to less confidence in you by the learners. To improve this situation, identify a mindset that will be more productive. If you could manage to adopt the mindset of, for example, 'this is going to be an opportunity to share some useful information with friends', then a completely different sequence of feeling, behaviour, and learners' response would be set in motion.

So the first step is to be aware of the mindset you may be unconsciously taking into the session. Review it and ask yourself if it is going to help your confidence. If not, select an alternative that will be more helpful and do whatever it takes to convince yourself of it.

Question 26: How do you keep your talk in the right order and should you use notes or prompt cards?

Clearly, you need to remember what you are going to say and in what order. However, it is also important to retain your connection with the group. Too much attention to a set of prompt cards, for instance, can lessen your ability to make eye contact with learners and can interrupt the flow of a talk.

PowerPoint slides, of course, can provide headings for you to follow. Again, be wary of looking at or even addressing the screen at the expense of maintaining contact with your audience.

Some lecturers write four or five headings and some subheadings boldly in marker pen on a page of A4 and have this where they can glance at it to keep them on track without losing their communication with the audience.

There is also the question of how rigidly you should stick to the script. John Shaw (2001) provides a useful analogy when he compares the lecturer to the jazz musician in his article, *How to turn thrifty lectures into rich jazz recitals*:

> When you attend such a (jazz) performance, you are conscious that the course of this music is not predetermined ... but you also realize that beneath the improvisation, there is a clear structure, which makes the experience coherent and understandable.
>
> Just as the jazz improviser states the theme at the beginning, explores its chords, produces alternative melodies and returns to it at the end, thus giving a more profound understanding of them, so the lecturer structures his or her performance to the same end.

One implication of this is that in preparation, 'prepare a lecture that can go down a number of alternative pathways' (Shaw 2001).

Question 27: How can I enjoy doing lectures more?

A possible answer to this may be found in the strengths-based model. This model holds that top achievers build their personal lives and careers on their talents and strengths. They learn to recognize their talents and develop them further. They find the roles that suit them best and they invent ways to apply their talents and strengths to their lives. As far as weaknesses are concerned, they manage rather than develop them. (Boniwell 2008: 80)

The model challenges two common assumptions:

1. Each person can learn to be competent in almost anything.
2. Each person's greatest room for growth is in his or her areas of greatest weakness. (Buckingham and Clifton 2005: 5)

The first step is to identify your strengths. Leslie Johnson (1996), in *Being an Effective Academic*, suggests that you can do this as follows:

1. Listen to your yearnings, they are a clue to a potential strength. Yearnings, or longings, can be characterized as the pull or attraction to one activity over another. They are often triggered when you see a performance or someone performing an activity and you say to yourself. 'I'd like to do that; I'd like to try that'. What do you long for?
2. What do you get a kick out of doing? It is unlikely you have a potential for a strength in some area if you don't get a kick out of doing its typical activities. If you are good at something but don't get a kick out of it, then this is not a strength. A strength feels good.
3. What have you learned quickly? A potential for strength is indicated by a desire to get on with it. You feel as though you know what to do. You are self-directed and learn quickly, managing books and experts as a learning resource.
4. Has someone you respect noticed a moment, an episode, of excellence in you? This is a clue to a potential strength.
5. When are you on automatic? When are you good, and unconscious of any joints in a flow of events? This is a clue to strength.

(Johnson 1996: 70)

Once you are clear about what your strengths are, you devote your energy at work and beyond to putting yourself in situations where you can draw on your strengths and excel, enjoy, and learn.

The complementary directive to building on your strengths is to manage your weaknesses. You may be able to identify an area of weakness when you recognize that you are slow to learn, you are defensive, and lack interest and motivation. Strategies for managing weakness include locating help and support, delegating, swapping or simply avoiding situations that emphasize your weakness.

The strengths-based model can be used by individuals in making plans for personal and professional development and can be used by managers looking to play to the strengths of their team. The most common objection, of course, is that this prevents you from trying something new and developing new skills.

Incidentally, the principles behind this have been proposed as the basis of an alternative approach to study skills in higher education. This suggests that the role of the study skills adviser should not be remediation but should instead be in helping learners identify the strengths in their existing study skills and maximizing their use of these (Schreiner and Anderson 2005). A book entitled *Teach with Your Strengths* applies the ideas to school teaching in the USA (Liesveld and Miller 2005).

If the principles behind this could be used to answer the question above, the response would be, you might enjoy your work more, get more satisfaction from it, and be more effective if you built on your strengths. Instead of attempting to become the well-rounded teacher, capable of using a range of techniques and materials, identify what you are good at – the parts where you excel and crucially which you enjoy and then seek to develop yourself further in these strengths. At the same time, identify your weaknesses and manage them.

For example, if you enjoy and know that you excel at storytelling (Question 21), look to use this technique for longer and more often as the framework for your lectures. If at the same time you always feel barely competent at creating and using PowerPoint slides, minimize your use of them or don't use them at all or, if you must, at least find a colleague who can create them or help you create them. Revel in your strengths, don't waste time working on your weaknesses. You will enjoy lectures more and, if the theory works, you will excel and be more effective.

Question 28: How do you make the same topic interesting for yourself as a teacher if you are regularly covering the same lecture?

I have met many lecturers who ask this question. Often they have to deliver the same session several times in a week. They often comment that they find the repetitions less interesting and they tend to go on 'automatic' and are less engaged.

Broadly, there are two options to maintain your interest. First, you can make changes to the sequencing of the content or the way in which you present it. Of course, it is important to attempt to ensure that all learners have the same experience and none are disadvantaged by being given less or different information. Making changes to the sequence or method of presentation should help keep you alert and therefore more likely to enjoy the learners' attention.

A second option is to design the session so that a portion of it will always be unpredictable. This should still be confined to changes in the sequence rather than the content. Here are two examples.

1. Use a variation of the idea described in Question 18 for generating questions. Gather questions about the topic at a midway point in the lecture. Read out and answer those questions that fall under the content planned for the second half of the session. In other words, cover the same content as you might have planned, but in response to 'live' questions.
2. Select a portion of the session in which the content items do not have to be presented in a fixed order. Let the group know what the items are, and ask them to choose which item to deal with first. You deal with their first choice; then they choose what goes next – you deal with that, and so on. This could be done as one PowerPoint slide with the title of each item on, where clicking on that title will lead you to the detail of that item.

Question 29: How can I develop my question-and-answer techniques to guide a student to a developed response?

Whenever you ask a question of a learner or group of learners or when you respond to a learner's question or comment, you really need to know what you are out to achieve. Some teachers' questions are used almost exclusively for testing understanding or recall – leading to teachers being described as the only people who ask questions when they already know the answer. This is one use of questions.

If you want to use questions in this way, or indeed to develop learners' understanding, Bloom's taxonomy (see Question 7) provides a useful framework for determining different types of question according to what you want the person answering the question to demonstrate. The following are the kinds of question that fall under each of Bloom's original six categories:

Knowledge
Questions aimed at recalling factual information:
Who, what, when, where? Can you list, define, describe?

Comprehension
Questions aimed at reformulating or explaining existing knowledge:
Can you compare, contrast, explain, differentiate between?

Application
Questions aimed at applying or using knowledge in new situations or problems:
How would you? What would you do in this situation?

Analysis
Questions aimed at analysing assumptions, reasons or evidence:
What are the assumptions, what's the evidence, how does this fit together?

Synthesis
Questions aimed at the creation of new ideas, concepts or plans:
Can/how would you create, formulate, design, plan, develop?

Evaluation
Questions involving making judgements on the basis of standards, criteria, rules or the critical evaluation of evidence:
Can you judge, defend, evaluate the evidence for, justify, appraise?
                                        (adapted from Exley and Dennick 2004: 44)

Four common errors to avoid when asking questions are:

- asking ambiguous questions;
- asking too many questions at once;
- asking a question and answering it yourself;
- not giving time for a response.

Once a learner has answered a question, you should also be wary of ignoring it or failing to build on it. Indeed, when a learner answers a question, makes a comment or asks a question, the automatic response of most teachers is to answer the question or confirm whether the answer/comment is accurate or not. Remember you have many more options, according to what you want your response to achieve. Some of the responses below would be suitable for the person who asked Question 29 in the first place:

- add information
- make a connection
- correct misunderstanding
- redirect the question
- ask for justification
- ask for elaboration

- offer advice
- ask for an example
- agree
- defer – suggest dealing with it later
- be devil's advocate
- simply welcome the comment and thank the contributor

Which of these options you use will depend on what you are seeking to achieve for this learner and indeed for the others. Do you want them to explore their opinions further, do you want to support them in their view, do you want to expose the fallacy in this viewpoint, do you want to reassure them? These are just some of the intentions you may have when responding

---

Task 9

Next time you have to respond, make a note of the learner's comment, answer or question and how you respond. Later run through the different responses you might have made.

Question 30: How can you make an effective ending – when you get to your last slide?

This question does assume slides will be used and that one will accompany the end of the session. If you do use slides, think about whether you want to display one as you end or if you wish to finish with the audience's attention fixed on you with no distractions. Plan for how you are going to end, ensure that the ending is purposeful, and make sure you leave the right amount of time for it – not having to sacrifice it if you fall behind schedule. Here are your options.

If you do use slides:

- Give a summary of the session.
- Revisit the learning objectives and confirm how each has been dealt with.
- Use a quote to make a conclusion.
- Show a picture which sums it up.

If you don't use slides:

- Confirm how any items, queries, loose ends from the session will be followed up.
- Confirm your contact details for any follow-up questions.
- Get some feedback from the learners about their whole experience of the session. For example, with a group of a suitable size you can use a round (see Question 6).

Also, if you are seeing the group again:

- Confirm/set the task that is to be completed before next time.
- Explain about and, if possible, enthuse about what's next.
- Get some feedback from them about their understanding (see 'The muddiest point' in Question 6).

Try to avoid asking for 'any questions' right at the end. If most learners have no questions and see the session as over, they be less attentive, not to say restless and packed up and ready to run, while any questions are asked and answered. Such an activity, with the majority opting out, can weaken the impact of the ending.

4 Management

Question 31: How can I establish a 'baseline' (general reference point) of the students' knowledge at the beginning of a session?

Ideally, if you are meeting a new group and want to establish their level of existing knowledge, you could seek some information in advance by email or via a virtual learning environment. The fact that learners can respond directly to you without being inhibited by revealing their ignorance (or knowledge) publicly is a benefit of this approach.

If you are going to gather information when you meet, these are your choices:

- use a keypad system if you have one (see Question 21);
- ask for a show of hands;
- carry out a test;
- distribute a questionnaire/checklist;
- talk with the group.

Thomas Angelo calls these 'background knowledge probes' (Angelo 2003). Examples of the kind of multiple-choice questions you might want to use in some of the above formats are:

'In relation to a topic, please indicate if you:

Have never heard of this
Have heard of it, but don't really know what it means
Have some idea what this means, but are not too clear
Have a clear idea what this means and can explain it

In relation to a problem, choose from:

> I have no idea how to solve this problem
> I once knew how to solve problems like this, but have forgotten
> I think I could solve it, given enough time
> I'm sure I can solve it right now'

(Angelo 2003: 6, 7)

If you are going to have to wait until the first time you meet a group to take account of the starting point, then you have to have an adaptable plan for the session. If you do have people in the group who bring some relevant previous knowledge, it is worth acknowledging this and making a point of welcoming their contributions as they may enhance what you have to offer.

Angelo and Cross suggest making 'misconception/preconception checks'. They point out,

> the greatest obstacle to new learning often is not the learner's lack of prior knowledge, but, rather, the existence of prior knowledge … it's much harder for learners to unlearn incorrect or incomplete knowledge than to master new knowledge in an unfamiliar field.

(Angelo and Cross 1993: 132)

If this is the direction you want to take in establishing prior knowledge, clearly your first step would be to identify common misconceptions and preconceptions for your course in order to make these the focus for the kinds of inquiry outlined above.

Question 32: What if, due to multiple questions, the structure of the session is very behind? How can you get back on track?

Timing is perhaps the most frequently overlooked aspect of planning and delivery of sessions in higher education. However, it can be very difficult to get right and experienced lecturers still get it wrong.

Recognize from the start how much time you have and don't forget to let this inform your planning. When planning a session, estimate how many minutes each section will take. Be as realistic as you can when doing this, especially the parts when you are explaining to the group. Lecturers commonly underestimate the amount of time that explanations take. If you can, try rehearsing how long it takes to say what you have to say, without interruptions.

If you are planning an activity for learners, fix on a likely duration that is not so short that they do not become engaged, but not so long that they finish with time to spare and may feel bored or frustrated that they cannot carry on. If you have to err on one side, generally it is better to have not enough time rather than to have too much. Have an idea yourself of the time each slot might take and be as scrupulous as you can be about adhering to it.

Announce an approximate schedule at the beginning. In particular, promise that the session will finish no later than a certain time.

A related question was:

> 'In facilitating a discussion among the group or small groups, what's the best way to "rein" people in who are going off at a tangent because you need to keep to time and to the point?'

It is OK to cut short questions in the interests of sticking to time. It is acceptable to say, 'Let's have just one more question' or 'I'm sorry there isn't time to hear your question now'. So the answer to the question is, you have to cut short questions to stay on track.

However, if moving on to the next part of the session will clearly leave a significant part of the group puzzled or not having grasped what's been dealt with so far, you will need to rethink. There is no point in sticking to the schedule if a proportion of learners are disengaged through lack of understanding. This confirms the importance of monitoring your plan periodically as the session unfolds. You may need to remind yourself what is most important from your plan, what can be postponed or made available online. Be ready to revise your plans as you progress. It is important to let the group know if there is a change of plan from what you initially promised. If you see time is running out, be wary of racing though a lot of material near the end after losing time and doing it such a way that it is meaningless.

Question 33: Do you have any advice for keeping a class focused while only one or a small group of them is feeding back from an activity?

Here is a very common scenario in higher education. Imagine the class has divided up into groups for a lengthy activity, which involves each group suggesting a solution to a problem or making a design or plan. The activity is completed and each group has to present their findings to the rest of the group. Say there are seven groups. Each takes five minutes to report back by displaying a piece of flipchart paper with their ideas on. At its worst this turns into death by flipchart. The average learner in the room spends most of thirty-five minutes:

- being passive and silent;
- listening to a number of ill-prepared summaries;
- not always being able to read what is on the flipchart as it is badly presented;

- not always being able to hear the presenter because of their lack of skills in presentation;
- hearing the same points made by different groups;
- resenting that one group has gone on for ten minutes without the teacher intervening;
- resenting that the last group has only two minutes and there is no time for a summary or guidance from the teacher.

These are all of the worst things that can happen to make this something other than a learning experience. If you as a teacher must use this activity, make sure that feedbacks are timed (e.g. two minutes each), make this clear and don't allow anyone to overrun, cutting them short if necessary. A couple of better ideas are:

1. Use a *crossover* as in Question 20. Each person from each original group has to feedback on their ideas to a new group comprising representatives of all of the other original groups.
2. A *graffiti poster tour*. Each group prepares its findings/ideas on a flipchart and displays them round the room. Ask learners to get into pairs and tour the room with a flipchart marker pen. Their brief is to look at each poster other than their own and write on it. They can write two things – constructive comments or questions that they think it would be useful for the group that created the poster to consider. When the tour is complete, each group retrieves their poster and discusses their response to the comments. Of course, you can review the posters too and provide summary guidance after the activity.

Both of these ideas should keep everyone involved all of the time.

A related question was:

> 'How do you take feedback from buzz groups to the wider group or do you just let it be?'

There are two points to make:

1. Think about what the experience would be for the whole group if all buzz groups reported back; avoid the situation as described above.
2. Ask yourself why you used the buzz group in the first place and if it was to get learners talking, thinking, problem-solving, and so on, then recognize that that has been achieved and that there is no need to report back.

Question 34: My course puts students into action learning sets. Would it be more useful to mix them into different groups regularly?

The answer to this question is brief but I want to take the time first to clarify what is meant by the term 'action learning set'. It is often incorrectly used to describe a small number of learners working as a group. It has a much more specific meaning than that. Action learning sets are often used in higher education and in other contexts too, for instance as a vehicle for professional development at work.

Normally, there are between four and six learners in a set. The set meets to assist its members in progressing with their projects or solving their particular work- or study-related problems. In a meeting, each member has an allocated amount of time. In that time, they can use the other members of the set to assist them with their project or problem. For instance, a member can explain where they are with a project and begin to explore the next step to take or any hurdles to overcome. The job of the other set members is to listen and to assist. They may, for instance, ask questions intended to provoke the member to reflect, they may provide advice or they may propose alternative courses of action. At the end of the allocated time slot, the member should have learnt from the opportunity to think out loud and from the support of the other members. Usually, the member makes a brief summary of their action plan arising from the discussion and the focus moves to another member.

For a set to operate effectively, agreement needs to be made on the rules of procedure and a deliberate review undertaken by the set at the end of a meeting to see if the set performed well. Rules for operation will look something like this:

- The time available is shared out equally or as agreed between members.
- Each member takes it in turn to present/explain their problem/task to the group.
- Group members devote their energies to assisting the person in exploring options and they are supportive but challenging where appropriate.
- Each person has to conclude their own slot with a clear resolve/action plan.

It is essential that the ground rules for operation of the set are agreed and adhered to by members. It is important that the group strives to maintain a positive, cooperative atmosphere.

Three roles need to be allocated:

- A chair who keeps time.
- A note taker who keeps a brief summary (not formal minutes) for the next meeting.
- A reporter who participates fully but also monitors and reports on how far the group stuck to the guidelines. The reporter initiates the review at the end of the meeting when the set in effect self-appraises.

Individuals who have had a positive experience of being in an action learning set cite the method as being an extraordinarily powerful means of learning. Others have had disappointing or frustrating experiences in sets. This is usually because rules were not made clear and adhered to by everyone and/or because there was no review by the set of its operation. In short, adherence to the process is key to success. More detail on action learning sets can be found in *Action Learning* by Ian McGill and Liz Beaty (2001).

Question 34 asks about changing the composition of action learning sets. If the questioner's use of the term 'action learning sets' was accurate, they should recognize that fixed membership of the sets is a prerequisite for their successful operation. If the questioner's use of the term just referred to groups assembled in order to carry out a brief task or activity, then it can be very helpful to vary the composition from task to task.

Of course it's OK for learners to form their own groups, although over a period of time they may well gravitate towards the same set of friends and familiarity can prevent open discussion, exploration, challenge, and they can collude in non-compliance with the task.

If you wish to ensure a change in the composition of groups, you could just say 'please get into groups of three and make sure you join with people who are not currently sitting at your table/in your row', or 'Make sure it is someone you have not worked with yet'. Or, you can quickly give each person a number and ask 'all of the ones to sit together, all of the twos ...', and so on. Some lecturers distribute Post-its® with different numbers on – 'sit with those who have the same number as you'. Directing a change of group composition can inject a new energy into the room and into the groups that form.

Question 35: How do we get the counterproductive stress versus productive challenge balance right?

This question arose following a discussion of Eric Jensen's distinction between 'positive stress' and 'negative stress' for learners. In *The Learning Brain*, Jensen writes:

Positive stress occurs when we:

- Have perceived a solution to a problem
- Have the ability to resolve a problem
- Have some control over a situation
- Get sufficient rest between challenges

The negative form of stress (distress) occurs when we feel stressed by some kind of threat, such as embarrassment, loss of prestige ... It also occurs when we feel helpless because we:

- Don't perceive a solution to a problem
- Lack the resources to solve a problem
- Have little or no control over a situation

(Jensen 1995: 228)

This balance is encompassed in Mihaly Csikszentmihalyi's concept of 'flow'. Flow is that state characterized by full absorption and complete concentration, when the individual is oblivious to external pressures of time, noise, and so on, and has no room for any other information: 'there is no space in consciousness of distracting thoughts, irrelevant feelings' (Csikszentmihalyi 1997: 31). Given that Csikszentmihalyi describes the state of flow as a 'magnet for learning' (ibid.: 33), it is worth exploring what conditions are conducive to flow and investigating whether these can be created for learners.

'Flow tends to occur when a person's skills are fully involved in overcoming a challenge that is just about manageable' (Csikszentmihalyi 1997: 30). If the challenge is too great, it can lead to frustration, worry, and anxiety – Jensen's 'distress'. If it is not great enough, then a sense of being relaxed can lead to boredom. But, 'When high challenges are matched with high skills, the deep involvement that sets flow apart from ordinary life is likely to occur' (ibid.: 30).

This alignment of the challenge with skills is one necessary condition for flow. Further conditions are a 'Clear set of goals that require appropriate responses' (Csikszentmihalyi 1997: 29) and to have immediate feedback provided by the activity – you are able see how well you are progressing. So, 'when goals are clear, feedback relevant, and challenges and skills are in balance, attention becomes ordered and fully invested' (ibid.: 31).

Other important factors include:

- the activity that the person is engaged in is intrinsically rewarding;
- there are no worries about failure;
- the person has some control.

While the concept of flow is an intriguing way to describe what Czikszentmihalyi calls 'excellence in life', prescribing how to induce flow in learners is a difficult task. To achieve it with the diversity of learners in one group would perhaps be impossible. What can be suggested is to strive to arrange learning experiences for your learners where:

- goals are clear
- feedback is available
- control is experienced
- the task matches the skills
- the reward is in the task
- there is no chance of failure

If you can create these conditions, there is the potential for learners to experience flow and, as Amy Fineburg suggests, 'if students can experience learning as flow, their enjoyment and intellectual stimulation about learning will likely be enhanced'. (Fineburg 2004: 202)

Question 36: How do you remember students' names?

Using names is important. Most learners respond well to the fact that you have identified them and this can affect their readiness to engage as well as the overall emotional tone in the session. Knowing names is also useful in assisting your control and direction of the session, particularly in small group teaching where people are making contributions and you want to indicate who should speak next. If you want to remember and use learners' names you can, but the key phrase is 'want to remember'. You have to be motivated to do this and plan for it. Make it an imperative, not an aspiration: 'I have to' not 'I would like to'.

Once you have the resolve, you need a plan to suit you. Of course, for very large groups this may be unachievable. However, if you are able to retrieve photos from the student record system, you could display them together with names, and begin to familiarize yourself with them.

With groups of thirty to forty, you can use other techniques. For example, on the first occasion you meet, arrange for everyone to state their name (or in a smaller group be introduced by someone else as part of an icebreaker) to introduce themselves. Write each name down and simultaneously use it, as in, 'Thank you Kerry'. Arrange for the group do be doing an activity shortly afterwards that does not require your involvement and then take the time to look at each individual in turn and see if you can remember their name. Practise saying it silently while looking at them. Take every opportunity to use names in the session.

Whichever technique you use is secondary; the key thing is that you see the learning and use of names as essential and not just something to be hoped for. Just as you wouldn't contemplate getting ready for a session without preparing what you are going to say and what materials you will use, in the same way, if you believe it is important to hear, remember, and use names in a first session, you need to plan for how to do so.

5   Materials and equipment

Question 37: How can you make PowerPoint presentations engaging?

PowerPoint is a presentation software, created in the 1980s and in widespread use in teaching in higher education. In planning your session, one of the questions to ask is whether to use PowerPoint. I'll repeat that last phrase: whether to use PowerPoint. In other words, you don't *have* to use PowerPoint. This will come as a shock to some lecturers who behave as though persistent use of PowerPoint were written into their contract. Some lecturers and learners respond to the absence of PowerPoint in a session as though it was an absence of oxygen – how can it possibly go ahead? A PowerPoint dependency has sprung up. It has become a comfort blanket for lecturers and learners alike. Its presence can stop people thinking, as they are reassured by the fact that there is lot of information presented on the slides and they 'look professional'. Confirmation of this is evident when for some reason PowerPoint is not used – the addicts start to look ill at ease, fidget, and start to panic. So, it's worth saying again – you don't have to use PowerPoint.

The strength of feeling about the dangers of PowerPoint is reflected in titles of pieces that criticize it, such as *Death by PowerPoint* by Michael Flocker (2006) and *Is PowerPoint the Devil?* by Julia Keller (2003). Such criticism also brings forth eloquent, pithy denunciations:

> Think of it as technological cocaine – so effortless to embrace initially, so difficult to relinquish after that.
>
> (Keller 2003)

> Under the guise of empowering people to tackle the difficult act of public speaking, PowerPoint reduces it to the rhetorical equivalent of painting by numbers – not to mention reading out

words and phrases which the audience can perfectly well read for themselves.

(Naughton 2003)

PowerPoint allows speakers to pretend they are giving a real talk and audiences to pretend they are listening.

(Tufte 2006: 31)

The criticism is generally aimed at either or both of:

- the way in which the structure of the software embodies assumptions about how knowledge is structured;
- the way in which the software is used.

Edward R. Tufte, in *The Cognitive Style of PowerPoint*, asserts that 'PowerPoint is presenter-oriented, not content-oriented, not audience-oriented' (Tufte 2006: 4). He says, 'formats, sequencing and cognitive approach should be decided by the character of the content and what is to be explained, not by the limitations of the presentation technology' (ibid.: 6). In the same vein, Peter Norvig made a serious point comically by turning Abraham Lincoln's famous Gettysburg address into a PowerPoint presentation (see http://norvig.com/Gettysburg/).

In deciding whether to use it, your initial question should be, 'Will it help in achieving the specified learning objectives for the session?' If you have identified your session objectives, you need to decide what methods and materials will help the learners achieve those objectives. Ask yourself if there is anything to be gained by using PowerPoint slides during the session – perhaps a great deal, perhaps a little, perhaps nothing at all. Remember, too, that the use of PowerPoint almost always confirms that the learners' role is to be passive recipients of knowledge.

Apart from the objectives, your decision may be influenced by the expected behaviour in your department, by learners' expectations, and of course by what equipment is available and how much time you have for preparation.

If you want to transmit information, you have other options:

- say it
- write it on a whiteboard/flipchart
- put it on handout
- show it on a DVD
- make it available online

However, sometimes PowerPoint may be the best way to do this.

In planning a session that uses PowerPoint or for that matter any technology, make sure you have a contingency plan. Ask yourself, 'what would I do if there were a power cut?' If you are ready for this most extreme eventuality, it should cover the others.

If you are going to use PowerPoint, here are the key points to remember.

When preparing slides

- A general rule is to keep it simple and minimize their use. Let the technology serve the session not rule the session.
- Be wary of allowing the technology to override the content. Just because you can make words on slides appear from different angles and dissolve and reassemble and make noises while doing so doesn't mean that you have to do that.
- Use slides sparingly; always look to see if you can reduce the number of slides. It is likely you will have experienced overkill as a learner or audience member – don't forget what that was like.
- Determine the best balance of text and visuals within a show and within a slide; you might opt for exclusively one or the other.

When preparing text on a slide

- Take care not to use too many colours; text is normally better as dark on a light background – high contrast is best.
- Font size should normally be 24 point or more; think whether those at the back of the room will be able to see it. Don't worry about it being too big, but it can be too small.
- Commonly used fonts, which are all sans serif and therefore less likely to cause problems for those with a visual impairment, are Arial, Times, Trebuchet, and Verdana.
- Try to confine text to the top half or two-thirds of the slide because in a large group some learners may not be able to see the bottom of a slide.
- Don't clutter the slides. Use the guidelines six by six or at most eight by eight – words following a bullet point, bullets points per slide.
- PowerPoint templates invite you to use bullet points but you don't have to use them all the time – short sentences are allowed!
- Don't use all capitals and avoid italics.
- Be even more rigorous than usual in checking your spelling.
- Remember, if you have nothing to add to what is on your slides, what you really need is more preparation, more research, more knowledge.

When using PowerPoint

- Remember to consider not showing a slide when you start so that your learners' attention is on you.
- Let the learners know from the start whether the material on the slides is/will be available as a handout/online so that they know whether they need to make notes or not.
- If you want the learners to read and digest a slide, leave it on for long enough.
- Don't just read every word on the slides – learners find this tedious and patronizing.
- Make sure you know how to navigate to another slide out of sequence if you want to return to a previous slide or skip a few slides. When you are on 'slide show', press the number of the slide you want to go to and then press 'enter'.
- Be careful to maintain eye contact with the learners and not to address the slide. Be especially careful not to point at the slide on the monitor as though everyone can see it – easily done!
- If you are not able to advance slides with a remote, be wary of getting pinned down in the space by the keyboard, possibly behind a lectern – see how far you can move the keyboard.
- Don't leave a slide on when you have moved on to talk about something else or the group has started an activity. For this, when you are in 'slide show', you can bring up a black screen by pressing 'B' (press it again to return to the slide) or if you prefer 'W' to give a white screen. This does not work when you are not in 'slide show'.
- Sometimes a blank slide can be used instead of a flipchart or whiteboard just to record the learners' feedback comments or answers to questions.

Question 38: Not wanting to give the audience 'death by PowerPoint', do you think that graphs and visuals are good to break up bullet points?

Lee and Bowers (1997) studied a group of 112 university students to determine what combination of the following was most effective in aiding learning:

- reading text
- listening to spoken text
- looking at graphics

They found that the most potent combination was:

- listening to spoken text and looking at graphics

followed in sequence by:

- listening to spoken text, reading text, and looking at graphics
- reading text and looking at graphics
- listening to spoken text and reading text
- looking at graphics alone
- reading text alone
- listening to spoken text alone

If you accept these findings, you might consider using PowerPoint just for graphics, accompanied by your commentary and talk.

Question 39: What guidance do you have on the use of handouts?

When considering a handout, the following are the key questions to ask:

1. In what way will it help learners achieve the objectives? If it is not clear how it will help them achieve the objectives, then ask why you are using it.
2. Exactly how do you want learners to use it? There are usually two ways in which handouts help:

   - *Handouts that provide information about the content of the session.* In using a handout, decide whether you want the content of the session to be replicated, summarized, outlined or supplemented.
   - *Handouts that assist active or interactive learning.* These are often called worksheets, incomplete handouts or interactive handouts. These might include key information about the session but also will include tasks for learners. For example, there may be incomplete sentences, definitions, lists or formulae that learners will be directed to complete at a given time, questions to answer, problems to solve, or space to draw graphs, diagrams, flow charts or mind maps.

   In directing the use of such handouts, some of the guidelines in Question 15 for directing activities will apply – that is, ensure that the task is clear, the task is achievable, there is a clear outcome required, and there is a fixed time for the task.

3. How does it integrate with the structure and content of the session?
4. Should it have words and/or visuals?
5. How do you want the learners to access it – online or print copy available in the session?
6. When do you want the learners to access it – before/at the start of/ during /at the end of/after the session?
7. When do you want learners to use it? If you are distributing print copies during a session, it is worth considering how to do that most efficiently if you have a large group in a lecture theatre, to avoid wasting time while everyone waits for a copy. For instance, you might want to prepare piles for distribution in advance.
8. Is it up-to-date?
9. Have you attended to the quality and inclusivity of the handout?

A quality handout will:

- be attractive
- be clearly set out
- be well structured
- be written in language that is understandable
- have sufficient blank space for notes
- provide space for any tasks to be completed
- have clear instructions that are not liable to misinterpretation – it is worth testing them in advance

An inclusive, accessible handout will:

- have a sans serif font, e.g. Arial, Times, Trebuchet, Verdana
- be no smaller than 12 point
- avoid excessive underlining, capitals, and italics
- have good contrast between the font colour and the background colour
- be left-aligned, not justified
- not be too dense, avoiding long blocks of continuous text, making use of bullet points and lists where suitable
- use wide margins and spaces between paragraphs

10. Do your learners have expectations of what a handout is for? Does this handout match those expectations and, if not, are you going to explain this? For instance, some learners will see the handout as a substitute for attending the lecture or for being attentive in the

lecture. The learners may need direction in how and when to use a handout, including when it is appropriate to be attentive to the hand-out and when to you.

Task 10

Apply these ten questions to your last use of a handout.

6   Problems

Question 40: How would you encourage people to attend?

There are usually two categories of reason why a learner would not attend your session: personal reasons or they can't see any value in attending. Personal reasons include illness or other priorities and responsibilities related to, for instance, family or work. If they can't see any value in attending, this could mean one of two things:

1. *They do not understand the value in attending.* The learner may not realize that:

    - Studies show that attendance increases their chance of passing and gaining good grades. Newman-Ford et al. (2008) evaluated 22 Level 1 modules within four separate award programmes, using attendance data gathered and stored electronically. The results showed a strong, statistically significant correlation between learning event attendance and academic attainment.
    - There is the opportunity by attending to learn content that is relevant to the assessment.
    - There is explicit support and guidance in the sessions on the assessment requirements.
    - The content of the session will be of obvious and immediate use in the profession they are pursuing/already in.

    You may need to convey this value to them.
2. *Actually there* is *no value in attending.* For example:

    - Learners find the sessions monotonous with no chance to engage, find it difficult to maintain attention, and experience too much reliance on passive learning – a handout would be an effective substitute.

- Some or all of the content is not obviously related to the assessment and so the learner can get all the information they need for the assessment from attending just a few sessions.
- There is no catering for differing intelligences/learning styles (see Question 52).
- There is no variety in methods or materials.
- The sessions are not inclusive (see Question 51).

You may need to review your teaching.

Of course, you can explicitly link the assessment with attendance. There are two examples in Question 49. Here is a third:

At the end of the lecture, learners have the option to make summary notes on a card distributed by the lecturer, putting their name on the card. They hand these cards in on leaving the lecture theatre. The teacher has explained that they will have the cards returned to them for use in the end-of-module exam.

Tutors using Patchwork Text (see Question 49) report increases in attendance, presumably because learners know that in the session:

- they will get feedback on their ideas which they can then use in the final assessment;
- they will hear from others about what they will be doing for the final assessment;
- they will be engaged by the process of giving and receiving feedback.

Question 41: You feel or see you are losing the audience. How do you recapture or engage them again?

The response to this is the same as to another question:

'What do you do when you've tried everything and you still look out at a sea of blank faces?'

The first thing is to be careful not to 'plough on regardless'. This was a phrase used by a group of learners in feedback about their lectures. They said that some lecturers had a plan and stuck to it regardless, even when it should have been evident that many of the group were struggling, either to understand or to remain attentive.

One option if you have sufficient confidence and flexibility is to talk about it. If the group is small enough, you could say something along these lines:

> 'As I look around at your faces, I just can't tell how this is being received. Let me stop the session for a moment and ask you each to tell me this. What is the one word that sums up what you think or how you feel about the session so far? Maybe it is "puzzled", maybe "bored", maybe "OK", maybe "intrigued". It doesn't matter what you say and you also have the option to say "pass". Let's just go round the group'.

You could hear from a group of forty in two minutes. Don't immediately respond to any particular comment. Be careful not to pass judgement on anything that is said. Of course, if the answers are largely negative, you will want to find out more: 'Which parts are puzzling?', 'In what way is it repetitive?' If the responses are positive, it gives you the reassurance to continue. Whatever the responses, you may want to extend the questioning and enhance your picture of how the material is being received. What this can achieve is:

- you get a rough idea of the learners' response;
- the learners will know that you are interested in their response (and not ready to judge it);
- the activity in itself will be a break in the session and whatever the group says, attention will increase afterwards.

If you don't want to go that far, just acknowledge what you see and improvise an activity: 'Before I move on/as a lead-in to the next section, I would like you to do this'. Or, at worst, just take a five-minute break.

If things are really bad, any activity at this point will be better than continuing. While the activity is taking place or during the next break, review your plan for the remainder of the session and change it if necessary in light of the response. An engaged group with reduced content will produce more learning than a disengaged group with full content.

Question 42: What strategies can you use when you have tried a new technique for a break in a lecture and it goes wrong/doesn't work?

A similar question asked was as follows:

'If an interactive teaching session is not well received, at what stage do you give it up?'

There are two key things to attend to immediately:

1. Decide whether you want to acknowledge that the technique has not worked and to talk about it with the learners, asking them what didn't work, explaining how it was supposed to work, and so on.
2. Whatever it was that you wanted the learners to achieve by engaging in the activity, quickly decide on an alternative way of helping them to achieve it.

After the event, you need to identify exactly what went wrong and why, so as to do it differently next time or to scrap it. The reasons why a technique (not always a new one) does not work usually stem from faults in the design or faults in the implementation.

Design faults – check to see if the activity was:

- too complex
- too easy
- at the wrong time in the session/in the module
- not suitable for this size of group
- using unhelpful/unsuitable materials
- just not aligned with whatever objective it was intended to achieve

Implementation faults – check to see if:

- the introductory explanation was complete or clear enough
- the composition of groups was suitable
- the right amount of time was given for the task

If you are observing that the activity is not going well and the cause is your explanation, see if there is time to go over it again.

Once you have used an activity successfully, remember that you can't assume it will work every time. But every failure does provide you with an opportunity to improve if you are ready to acknowledge the failure and put your energies into learning from it.

Question 43: How to regain composure/confidence if things don't go well?

Question 42 was about a specific situation where things go wrong and the guidance given was to investigate what lay behind that. This question focuses more on your own reaction and feelings when something does go wrong.

Martin Seligman (2006) suggests a model to investigate how you respond to adversity. He uses the ABCDE model (adapted from psychologist Albert Ellis's ABC model) to explain one way in which you can deal better with setbacks. This is how it could apply in the situation raised in Question 42:

- **A** stands for *adversity* – those everyday setbacks that you experience. In this case, a technique has failed in a session.
- **B** stands for *belief* – that is, how you interpret the adversity, how you explain it to yourself. You may say to yourself: 'Clearly this failed because I gave a poor explanation. I am not good at explaining things and am a poor teacher. These kinds of activities will never work for me'.
- **C** stands for *consequence* – that is, the feeling you experience as a result of what you said to yourself in B. In this case, you could easily feel inadequate, frustrated, and incompetent.

Task 11: Part 1

Recall any slight adversity while teaching or in some other area at work recently. What was your 'belief' in response to that adversity – what did you say to yourself? What consequence resulted – how did your belief shape your feeling?

- **D** stands for *disputation* – this is where you return to B and try to take a more objective view:

  'Yes I did give a poor explanation, that's true. But I am certain that the activity was well-designed and in truth, it wasn't a disaster, just a mild disappointment and not the best use of those five minutes. If I had to explain it again, I think I know where I could improve it. I must recognize that everything else in the session has gone OK and in some places quite well. I suspect the learners were not as critical of the activity as I am being', and so on.

This more rounded view of the adversity does not turn it into something long-lasting and pervasive about you as a teacher.

- **E** stands for *energization* – this means that if you accept the disputation, then you will not experience the feelings brought on by B, which can take up a great deal of your energy and not assist you in continuing with the task in hand – that is, the remainder of the session. You will instead have the energy to concentrate on what needs to be attended to next. The different interpretation in 'D' leads to different feelings that are more likely to assist you in continuing.

Task 11: Part 2

What happened next in your example? Were the feelings at 'C' OK or did they leave you feeling defeated or demoralized? If the latter, what would your 'D' look like and how would it have affected your level of energy and readiness to pick up?

Seligman's model is based on two ideas: first, that feelings are powerful and can help or hinder our recovery from a setback; second, that most feelings are preceded by a thought or belief or interpretation. When encountering adversity, the key is the choice you make in how to interpret it. This will provoke feelings and some feelings are potentially disabling, preventing you from continuing effectively. The more you can interpret setbacks as temporary, particular to the situation and not necessarily always a result of some incompetence on your part, the more likely you are to recover quickly from them.

Question 44: How do you manage difficult students or groups?

I shall start to answer this by discussing lecturers' perceptions of difficult learners or groups and then go on to consider the following:

- general principles in responding to behaviour you perceive to be difficult;
- questions to help in learning from your experience of difficulties;
- guidance on how to prevent difficulties arising through curriculum design and delivery;
- a model for investigating your exchanges with learners.

One person's difficult learner

The initial problem in answering this question is that individual lecturers will have differing meanings for the phrase 'difficult students or groups'. Here are two examples of teachers' perceptions.

Parker J. Palmer tells a memorable tale of 'The Student from Hell' in which, as a guest lecturer, he focuses on one learner who appears to be completely disengaged, takes this as a comment on his teaching, and devotes all of his energies into getting that learner's attention (Palmer 1997: 40–47). In an opportunity to talk with the learner afterwards, he discovers that what was truly behind the learner's sullen disengagement was fear. Palmer says he was too concerned to see the learner as a comment on his own teaching to take the time to think more about the learner. 'I read that student not in the light of his condition but in the shadow of my own and my self-absorbed misreading led me into one of my lowest moments in teaching' (ibid.: 46).

On perhaps a more mundane note, a university professor tells me that he occasionally got into trouble as an undergraduate because of looking out of the window while the lecturer was speaking. He says it was his natural way of concentrating but that it was sometimes misinterpreted by his lecturers as disengagement. The term 'gaze aversion' has been used to describe this behaviour and it is acknowledged that it assists some people during difficult cognitive activity.

So the first thing in seeing difficult behaviour is to check your perception. How much is incontrovertibly 'difficult' and how much is interpretation on your part?

General principles

At the moment that you perceive a learner or whole group to be difficult, you will need to know what to do. It is not possible to prescribe here the exact words or behaviour you should draw on, as each situation and incident is unique. However, there are some general principles:

- Acknowledge the behaviour, don't ignore it.
- Speculate on what lies behind it – put yourself in their shoes – why is this happening?
- Don't exclude them.
- Attempt to turn negative energy into positive – there is energy behind the disruption; seek to direct that energy to a more positive purpose.
- Attempt to make them self-aware – they may not be aware of what they are doing and, more importantly, of its impact.
- Remind the learners of any required or agreed rules of behaviour.
- Don't take it personally.
- Look for a resolution that keeps everyone on track.

Learning from experience

If there was an incident and you didn't handle it too well, here's a checklist of questions to work through by writing down the answers and/or talking them through with a colleague to help you more fully understand what happened and perhaps to be better prepared next time.

- Select a difficult situation with a learner or group that you have experienced.
- Describe what happened. Don't make judgements yet or try to draw conclusions; simply describe. Make sure it is just facts – no inferences or assumptions.
- Describe how you felt at the time. Have you experienced these feelings before with learners or groups?
- What were you thinking to yourself during the incident that caused these feelings?
- Put yourself in the position of the difficult learner(s). What were they trying to achieve? What do you think lay behind what they said or did?
- Are there any alternative responses you could have made?
- Looking back, what sense can you make of the incident and your reactions?
- What conclusions can you draw about the incident and your reactions?
- If the same thing happened tomorrow:

  - Would it provoke the same feelings in you?
  - Would you respond in the same way?
  - If not, what would you do or say instead?
  - What would you be out to achieve by this?

- Look back at all of your answers above. What have you learnt from this exercise?

Check the curriculum design and execution

If difficult learners are a common experience, it is worth investigating possible causes of the disruption, which you may be able to anticipate. There is no excuse for behaving badly but there are things you might do or fail to do that make such behaviour more likely.

Lewis Elton has adopted a model developed by Frederick Herzberg in 1959 that was used to explain the causes of satisfaction and dissatisfaction at work and he has applied it to learners in higher education (Elton 1996). Herzberg identified two sets of factors. *Hygiene factors* need to be present to prevent workers experiencing dissatisfaction. These include working conditions, salary, and job security. However, although these prevent dissatisfaction, they do not themselves induce satisfaction. This depends on *motivation factors*, such as achievement, recognition, and responsibility.

Translating this idea to higher education, Elton suggests that the equivalent of hygiene factors is clear information about assessment. Learners need to know about what the assessment entails. This includes knowing what criteria will be used, what these criteria mean, and how they will be applied.

Herzberg suggests that motivation factors will not have an effect until hygiene factors have been attended to. Hygiene factors are a prerequisite to motivation factors being able to have an impact. In other words, any *intrinsic* motivation that the learners have to study will be affected by the presence or absence of clarity about the assessment requirements. Elton writes,

> extrinsic factors must be increased first, something that is likely to go against the common sense beliefs of most teachers whose strategy is usually to attempt to motivate unmotivated students by making the subject more interesting to them.

(Elton 1996: 65)

He suggests a grid (see Figure 5) that indicates the likely outcome in terms of learner behaviour according to what combination of extrinsic and intrinsic

Extrinsic Motivation	Favourable	Playing the system	Low commitment	High commitment
	Unfavourable	Despair	Withdrawal	Rebellion
		Negative	Positive-low	Positive-high
		Intrinsic Motivation		

Figure 5. Combinations of intrinsic and extrinsic factors.

(Adapted from Elton 1996: 64)

factors they experience. Note that the learner with high intrinsic motivation but lack of guidance about assessment may engage in 'rebellion'.

You may query the terminology that Elton uses for each of the six categories or indeed whether the formula is that precise, but it is certainly worth considering what can be done to give the learner a sense of security about assessment in order to influence their outlook on the course and the sessions. They will still have the anxiety about how well they perform in the assessment but they will be confident that they know what they are being asked to demonstrate.

Ways of developing this security and increasing levels of extrinsic motivation include:

- Specify the assessment criteria and ask the learners to use them to mark work, possibly from a previous year (as detailed in Question 11).
- Set a seminar activity, in which learners first mark their own draft assignment against the criteria and then, working in pairs, mark a colleague's work.
- Run an exercise for learners to generate criteria.
- Turn listed criteria into feedback sheets.

Exercises in marking can be a learning activity in their own right; learner-generated criteria can foster a sense of ownership. However, there are some potential dangers:

- Do not rely completely on extrinsic factors, otherwise learners' learning will be 'driven' by the assessment and they will simply *play the system*.
- Do not create a mismatch between what is tested (extrinsic factors) and what is seen to be valued (intrinsic factors). In extreme cases, this could lead to *rebellion*.
- Do not create a situation where your learners have little sense of achievement (low intrinsic motivation) and little idea of what is to be tested (low extrinsic motivation). This could lead to *despair*.

Strategies for developing intrinsic motivation have already been touched on in Question 11.

Other things you can do to make difficult behaviour less likely

1. Ensure variety in teaching and learning methods and include opportunities for active rather than passive learning to avoid boredom.
2. Make sure there is the opportunity for learners to voice anxieties or questions to avoid resentment.

3. Demonstrate empathy and show that when learners speak, you are genuinely listening and respecting their viewpoint, to avoid feelings of not being valued.
4. In responding to comments and questions, avoid the errors listed in Question 29.
5. Monitor your prejudices and preferences and check whether you are unconsciously treating individual learners or groups of learners differently on the basis of their appearance, attitudes or behaviours.
6. Give learners the opportunity to be at least slightly physically active in a session, subject to the constraints of the room and time. For example, moving to change groups or conducting a paired activity while standing rather than sitting.
7. Whenever possible acknowledge individuals, if only by eye contact, but preferably by name and where appropriate and possible acknowledge their previous contributions.
8. Acknowledge that each learner may have a different way of learning, which can result in differing behaviours in the class.
9. Put energy into developing a good relationship with your group by using strategies such as those above. Showing that you respect learners and that you have their best interest as learners at heart should have a strong influence on their perception of you and on their behaviour.

Investigating your exchanges with learners

Some lecturers have found the concepts of 'ego-states' and 'transactions' useful in investigating their exchanges with 'difficult' learners. These are part of the theory of transactional analysis created by Eric Berne.

An ego-state describes how you are thinking, feeling, and behaving at any one moment. There are three broad categories of ego-state. These are Parent, Adult, and Child. When you are in the Parent ego-state, you are thinking, feeling, and behaving in ways you associate with being a parent, which you absorbed in your very early years from those who were responsible for your upbringing. When you are using the Child ego-state, you are replaying the thoughts, feelings, and behaviours you recall from the years when you were a young child. When you are in the Adult ego-state, your thoughts, feelings, and behaviours are based on what is happening here-and-now, rather than your experiences of long ago.

There are two subdivisions of the ego-states Parent and Child: Controlling Parent/Nurturing Parent and Natural Child/Adapted Child. The relevant ego-states for this section are Controlling Parent and Adapted Child. Controlling Parent as you can imagine is made up of those parental thoughts, feelings, and behaviours that you associate with directing, telling and, indeed, controlling. They are an essential part of any effective parental role. The Adapted Child ego-state is always a response to parental expectations (as opposed to the Natural Child, which encompasses behaviour independent of such expectations). The Adapted Child can be, broadly, compliant or rebellious.

Transactional analysis suggests that the reason we inhabit a particular ego-state at any one time may be because we feel comfortable with it, because it confirms the view of the world we developed when a young child. Or it may be as a result of a *transaction* with someone else whereby their behaviour has triggered us to switch to a complementary ego-state.

As a teacher, it is appropriate to inhabit the Controlling Parent ego-state for some of the time, as you direct learner activities and to some extent behaviour. Problems can arise, however, if a learner's behaviour that arises from the rebellious, sulking part of their Adapted Child triggers an unconscious response from your Controlling Parent. Because, in that response, you have addressed their Adapted Child, they will see no reason to come out of it. They will have been encouraged to look to you to join in with more of the Adapted Child–Controlling Parent transactions that they crave, and so will push you into the Controlling Parent role.

This model describes what some new lecturers have told me about their experiences. They have assumed their learners would exhibit reasonable, 'adult' behaviour and have been taken aback by uncooperative responses from some learners, which they see as 'childish'. The lecturers are disappointed and describe themselves as having to behave more like a 'schoolteacher', having to discipline and control their learners.

The key is to be aware of these invitations to be excessively Controlling Parent and to exert more control over the transaction by ignoring the Adapted Child in your learner and addressing their Adult from your Adult. Continue with your expectations of reasonable behaviour and give matter-of-fact responses, not feeding the learner's Adapted Child.

Question 45: How do I stop myself 'waffling' when I have run out of things to say?

Have a plan for what to do in this eventuality. Options include:

- Look back at the idea of 'must do, should do, could do' (see Question 3). Make sure that when planning for all three that the 'could do' material takes you well beyond the allotted time. If you do need more to say, draw on this portion.
- Have an extra activity planned that will consolidate learners' learning but which is not indispensable.

- If you used the questions activity earlier (see Question 18), return to some unanswered questions. Or, redistribute those questions to the group (size permitting) and ask them in pairs/threes to begin to try to answer them.
- Do two/three/four/five minutes each way (see Question 7).
- Give more details on the following session(s).
- Reinforce how the assessment relates to the topic you have just covered.
- Or ... finish! There are unlikely to be any complaints.

Question 46: How can you deal with a situation when you are asked a question you don't know an answer to?

If you are asked a question to which you do not know the answer, it is unwise to pretend that you do. You have to confidently say that you do not know, welcome the opportunity to find out, and then confirm when and by whom the answer is going to be discovered. So, having said, 'I don't know', your possible responses include:

- 'Does anyone else know?'
- 'Would you like to look that up for next session?'
- 'You should be able to find the answer in/at ...'
- 'Let's find the answer online now'.
- 'Let me find out for you and put it on the virtual learning environment/tell you next week'.

This situation touches on the very definition of what your role is and what you want to encourage your learners to do. Is expertise in the subject all that you offer them? Are you the sole source of information for your learners? Do you want them to be capable of finding information themselves? In short, it is OK to say 'I don't know'. Of course, if it happens too often you lose credibility and you may wonder if you are teaching the right subject.

A related question was:

> 'What should I do if a student asked a question and I could not understand him?'

Whenever any learner asks a question there are good reasons for you to repeat it. In a large group it is important that everyone hears the question and sometimes it will be necessary for you to repeat it. Often, it is useful to repeat it to check that you have heard and understood it correctly: 'Let me check, your question is ...'. If you have not understood what the learner has said, it is OK to ask them to say it again. If you still do not understand the question, you must enter into dialogue with the learner. 'So, are you saying ... ?', 'Do you mean ... ?', to get clarification before you attempt to answer.

Question 47: How to deal with students who ask non-relevant questions, i.e. not related to the topic being presented?

The following question was in the same vein:

> 'How can you continue to question a learner who has given an incorrect answer?'

You have to be clear what you are out to achieve when you respond to a question or answer from a learner that is wrong or appears to be irrelevant to the topic. I hope you would want to achieve three things:

1. Not to discourage the learner, or indeed others in the group, from asking or answering a question again.
2. Not to pretend that the question is relevant or that the answer is right.
3. To correct any evident misunderstanding on their part.

I would suggest it is important to be honest but respectful in your response, and so be attentive to your manner and your choice of words:

*   'In fact the answer is ...'
*   'Tell me your thinking behind that'
*   'What makes you say that?'
*   'This is a very common misunderstanding'
*   'Is anyone ready to agree or disagree with X's answer?'

When responding to an irrelevant question, it may even be OK to answer it briefly and follow with, 'but what we're talking about today is ...', or simply to say 'there is not time to answer that or open up that topic now. What we need to focus on is ...'.

Question 48: What is the best way or format for teaching about a subject you do not know a great deal about?

A spontaneous response to this question would be, 'Don't!' However, Therese Huston emphasizes the advantages of teaching what you do not know (Huston 2009). She states that although lecturers frequently have to teach outside their area of expertise, it is seldom talked about, still less written about. She is not talking about working in another discipline, but rather when you are asked to teach on a subject you are unfamiliar with but which is related to your expertise.

What looks initially like an unpromising situation can advantage learners. She writes, 'It may not be the world's most comfortable teaching, but students can learn as much, if not more, than they can in classes where you're teaching from the core of your expertise' (Huston 2009: 8). She suggests the 'content novice' has three potential advantages over the 'content expert':

1. You are more likely to have a realistic assessment of what the learners can achieve. Being new to the topic yourself, your sense of what it takes to grasp the key points is still fresh and you can empathize with the learners' perspective.
2. Your explanations for problem-solving are likely to be more basic and concrete because you have only recently learned to solve the problem yourself.
3. You are more likely to promote deep approaches to learning in your learners because you are less likely to include the content overload that encourages a surface approach. Your limited knowledge means you are forced to think about tasks that will assist the learners in absorbing the core knowledge.

(Huston 2009: 45–55)

These three advantages do not address directly the original question but begin to suggest the approach to take. Don't attempt to take on the role of subject expert, which you cannot be. This means you have to see your value to the learners in terms of how you can help them learn rather than as the source of extensive information. At the same time, look for ways to make the experience interesting for you. So:

- Be realistic about what can be achieved given your starting point.
- Pick on an aspect of it that interests you.
- See what there is in the topic that can relate to what you do know about and focus on that.
- Limit how far you aim to go into the topic in the session. Take the time to grasp the key points and turn those into your learning objectives. Arrange an activity that enables learners to apply, rehearse or explain those key points.

It is not just the learners who might benefit. Therese Huston suggests four advantages for the lecturer that can result from this experience. There is the opportunity to:

- learn something new and interesting;
- connect with faculty outside your department;
- broaden your curriculum vitae;
- develop a new area of research.

(Huston 2009: 31–34)

To which I would add:

- develop confidence and resourcefulness as a teacher;
- perhaps illuminate your own area of expertise, if the topic you are teaching is connected.

Overall, consider seeing this as an opportunity to be embraced rather than a commitment to be endured.

7   Outside the lecture

Question 49: How do I get students to look at the material between sessions?

The question of what learners do with independent study outside of contact time frequently receives less attention than it deserves. However, if contact time represents a small part of the learner's study week, it is worth considering how much direction learners require for the time when they are studying independently.

It is still the case that when designing a module, once the outcomes and assessment have been determined, lecturers put most of their energy into planning what happens in the time when lecturer and learner are in contact, whether that be in lectures, seminars, tutorials, workshops or labs. It is not uncommon for this contact time to form a small percentage of the total assumed study time for a learner on a module. For instance, a learner's thirty hours' attendance is just 20 percent of a total allocated study time of 150 hours. If asked, a lecturer might have only a broad idea of what should be happening in the other 80 percent, such as reading or planning for assessment.

In designing a module, perhaps it is best to start with the anticipated total study hours for each learner and ask how far you can direct that time. Purposeful independent learning (that is, independent of the lecturer) can be very productive, more so than the often passive learning that occurs in the lecture. Therefore, the question of what should be happening in independent study time deserves at least as much of the lecturer's energy as what happens during contact time.

Perhaps the notion that independent learning supports what happens in contact time should be reversed and class contact time should be perceived as the support necessary for effective independent learning. What methods can be used in class to support high-quality independent learning? The teaching can be designed around the desired independent study, not the other way round.

In particular, now that information can be so readily accessed online, such as through video lectures or podcasts, there is less justification for using contact time for the transmission of information from lecturer to learners. Class contact hours can instead be used to:

- develop project ideas;
- focus on the outcomes of independent work;
- respond to questions and problems that have arisen in the independent work;
- focus on application of knowledge to problems or scenarios;
- give more attention to assessment briefings.

This approach forces the lecturer to think about how they would like the learners to work independently and guides the learners in terms of what is expected of them. It is instructive to conceptualize the task as one of generating effective independent learning hours and thinking of the teaching input necessary to achieve this.

Virtual learning environments are still liable to be used merely as an archive for course materials, rather than to complement what happens in contact time. Most virtual learning environments do offer a variety of activities, such as wikis, forums, and quizzes, for use as directed study tasks between sessions.

> making teaching work now extends to making well-informed decisions about what exactly is best learned by students working alone with online technology and what is best reserved for face-to-face interactive contexts.
>
> (Race and Pickford 2007: 101–102)

Teachers need to take the opportunity in lectures to show learners how what they are doing there links to what they should be doing outside of the session, such as in the virtual learning environment.

Even with a holistic module design, some learners will work more or less and some will skip the lectures or read less. The motivated learners are likely to do the required inter-session directed tasks and possibly more. Others may perceive that there is no penalty for not doing such work and that they can get by without it. Your challenge, then, is to identify incentives for the less motivated learners to engage with the module material between taught sessions.

The two likeliest forms of incentive are *assessment* and *peer pressure*. Here are two examples:

First, a lecturer in property valuation on a BSc (Hons) Real Estate degree gives his students 'random mini tests' at the start of some sessions. The results from these tests count for a percentage of the students' final grade. The lecturer does not state in advance which of the sessions will include tests, only that the subject matter of the test will be the previous week's lecture and seminar. The benefits he describes include:

- promotes punctuality;
- reduces disruption by latecomers;
- improves attendance in both lectures and seminars;
- creates anticipation and a sense of fun;
- encourages and motivates ongoing study/revision;
- produces an improvement in module pass rate;
- provides useful feedback, early on, for both students and tutor;
- supports progression statistics and attendance monitoring.

Second, students on an engineering course needed more practice in working through numerical problems.

> The solution they adopted was to set the students problems on a regular basis to solve in their own time, and to allow 20 minutes at the start of certain lectures for these to be marked. This is done by rows of students swapping work; the lecturer then leads them through a model solution. Although 170+ students are involved they have become increasingly efficient at doing this and needed less time – only 7 minutes on one occasion. It was made a course requirement that all students had to have attempted 50 problems over the term (in order to be eligible to sit the end of term exam) but marks did not count. It would therefore have been possible for students to only make a perfunctory attempt at each problem and get them all wrong and still be able to sit the exam. But this did not happen. The students did take the problems seriously, presumably because they did not know which of their class mates would be marking their work and they did not want to be 'shown up'. And the performance in the exam has improved staggeringly.
>
> This is because not only are they getting increased practice in undertaking problems, and the associated feedback, but they are also benefiting from:
>
> - seeing the preferred solution, with the weighting of an examination marking scheme explained;
> - seeing the variety of approaches taken by their peers;
> - having to judge the degree to which the work of their peers does or doesn't meet the requirements of the marking scheme.
>
> (Rust 2001: 14)

Simply put, if you want learners to work on material before a session, consider how that work can be rewarded by being linked to summative assessment. In the second example, it seems that the prospect of failing in front of peers was an added incentive.

Work between sessions is an integral part of patchwork text assessment. The patchwork text was the focus for a three-year multi-disciplinary research project involving Anglia Polytechnic University, Cambridge University, and Nottingham Trent University. The findings were presented in a national conference in June 2003 and in a special edition of the journal *Innovations in Education and Teaching International* in May 2003.

Patchwork text assessment is characterized by learners preparing short pieces of work (patches) at regular intervals during a module. Each learner has the opportunity to provide feedback on others' patches and to receive feedback on their own. They use the patches, and perhaps the feedback they receive, in the final summative assessment.

The following is an example of how patchwork might operate. The assessment for a module is a 3000-word essay. The module runs for fifteen weeks. At intervals during the module, say every two or three weeks, learners are required to prepare a patch – a short piece of writing of five hundred words each. After being given the brief for the patch during a taught session, they are expected to bring copies of their completed patch to the session two weeks later. In this session, time is set aside for learners in groups of between four and six to hear or read each others' patches and to give feedback on them. No grades are awarded for this work. When it is time for the final essay submission, learners are expected to use their patches in putting together the 3000 words. They will literally cut and paste all or some of their earlier pieces and add words in order to 'stitch' them into a coherent whole for the assessment.

The components of this process that are variable are:

- the nature of the final assignment;
- the number of patches;
- the nature of the patches;
- how the patches are submitted and discussed – they could be done online;
- the extent to which patch submission is monitored by the teacher.

The essential components, which should not be varied, are:

- no summative assessment of patches;
- peer feedback on patches;
- the need to include patch extracts or whole patches in the final piece;
- a clear link between the patches and the final assessment task.

Results can be startling. Colleagues report increased motivation of learners, higher attendance, and better completion rates. A key influence on this is the fact that although the content of a patch is contributing towards the final assessment, the patch cannot be failed. They are a low-risk activity for the learner. They do present a great learning opportunity.

In changing a module to patchwork text assessment it may not be necessary to change the summative assessment. What you are introducing is direction to the learners on work to do during and outside of contact time that will assist them in preparing for that assessment.

The key steps in planning for patchwork are:

- be clear about what is being assessed in the final assessment;
- decide what each patch will deal with and how it contributes to the final assessment;
- decide the sequence of patches;
- determine the content and sequence of taught sessions so that they prepare for the patches.

Other questions to ask include:

- How will I integrate the patches with the module structure?
- How will I design the patches?
- How do I sort the groups for sharing the patches?
- What are the criteria for giving feedback on the patches?
- What are the briefing and criteria for the final piece?
- How will I structure the process of giving feedback in groups?
- How do I prepare the learners for the process of sharing patches and giving and receiving feedback?
- Do I monitor the submission of patches and, if so, how?

Examples of patches include:

- Reflect on what you learned about the practical exercise/evaluative exercise/the content in last week's session.
- Identify an interesting topic for your research and how you might go about researching this area.
- A critical, evaluative or analytic personal account of a piece of subject specialized published writing.
- A report about your own project.
- A journal of ongoing thoughts and feelings about your learning from the module.
- A critical incident analysis.
- A case study problem.
- Data analysis.
- A report on a visit.

- Write an explanation of your own professional practice from the point of view of one of your own clients/service users.
- An explanatory defence of an action research proposal for a local research ethics committee.
- A review of literature.
- Explain a difficult concept in the form of a letter to a friend.
- Draw a mind map.

The following are typical of comments made by learners about their experience of patchwork text:

> 'There is less pressure at the end of the semester; you can "check" on your learning during the course'.

> 'It was useful because it was easier to do pieces on different things over two-week periods rather than do them all right at the end'.

> 'Breaking the assessment task down allows easier understanding – greater in-depth knowledge of individual parts of the course through the patches'.

> 'The group sessions were good, got people talking rather than sitting there and not really knowing what to say'.

> 'Peer review was quite useful as it gave us the opportunity to share our work and get feedback from others so we could compare our work'.

Task 12

Could an existing assessment of yours be turned into a patchwork assessment? If that is a possibility, go though the steps above to begin to help you explore how this could be done.

Question 50: What are the mechanisms we can use to get or motivate students to 'digest'?

This question followed an explanation of Phil Race's model of learning (see Question 11), in which one of the key components necessary for effective learning is the opportunity to 'digest' (Race 2005: 24). This means having the time to absorb new learning, to make sense of it, and to understand it fully before moving on.

The idea of digesting resonates with Guy Claxton's analysis in *Hare Brain, Tortoise Mind* (Claxton 1998). He suggests that we have three kinds of intelligence – wit, d-mode, and wisdom. *Wit* is that instantaneous response where you act before thinking such as when you reach to catch something you have dropped or put the car brakes on to avoid a collision. *D-mode*, short for deliberation mode, is what we normally think of as intelligence that is measurable, an observable readiness to analyse, problem-solve, discuss, and deliberate. It is deliberate conscious thinking, the sort that teachers in higher education seek to promote in their learners. But there is also *wisdom*. This is arrived at intuitively and is the work of the unconscious mind. It is what emerges when you have literally 'had time to sleep on it'. It is helped by not trying hard to think about something or solve a problem. As Alexander Pope said, 'Some people will never learn anything because they understand everything too soon'.

Here is some of the vocabulary that Guy Claxton draws on when trying to convey the workings of wisdom:

> ruminating, less purposeful, less deliberate, less clear-cut, playful, leisurely, dreamy, mulling things over, contemplative, meditative, pondering, fragmentary, apparently aimless, relaxed, unquestioning, patient, slower, mistier, unconscious, loafing
>
> (Claxton 1998: 2–13)

Of course, these words do not sit easily in a higher education culture with fixed outcomes and a sense of pressure of time. Perhaps wisdom does not lend itself easily to being nourished by a higher education pedagogy, although a method such as storytelling, for example (see Question 22), is likely to assist this process as it engages both the conscious and unconscious mind. But Claxton asserts that 'thinking slowly is a vital part of the cognitive armamentarium. We need the tortoise mind just as much as we need the hare brain' (Claxton 1998: 2).

However, you might encounter problems on several fronts if you urge your learners to go away and 'ruminate'. Perhaps the best solution to draw on in helping your learners to digest is the notion of the 'self-convincer' (Jensen 1995: 175–176) derived from neuro-linguistic programming, which recognizes that the learner may have to validate their learning on a number of occasions and/or in a number of different ways before they *really* know something. This is bound up with the notions of 'ownership' and constructivism. In other words, some learners will 'know' something when they have had a chance to do one or more of the following:

- try it out
- explain it to another

- write a reflective piece for themselves about it
- draw it as a picture
- turn it into a diagram or equation
- plan to use it

It is worth alerting learners to the fact that they do not *have to* 'get it' immediately. Maybe they can forget about it for now and come back to it. The need to digest supports the case for not getting too prescriptive about when objectives are achieved.

8 Diversity

Question 51: How do you ensure that whatever strategy you choose, it is fully inclusive?

Being inclusive in your teaching means minimizing the risk of any aspect of the learning experience resulting in a learner or group of learners being disadvantaged. For example, asking learners to read a previously unseen quantity of material in a teaching session may disadvantage a learner with dyslexia, speaking too quickly and using colloquialisms may disadvantage a learner whose first language is not English, directing learners to move to change groups may disadvantage someone who has problems with mobility.

Discussion of inclusive teaching normally includes reference to learners with specific disabilities such as dyslexia, hearing impairment or visual impairment as well as learners from different cultures. Writers on teaching inclusively always stress that much of what is recognized as good practice in teaching is by nature inclusive. In the introduction to *Inclusivity and Diversity*, Sue Grace and Phil Gravestock declare that they are using the terms inclusion and diversity:

> in their broadest sense to mean issues relating to all students and to types of teaching and learning that fully and equitably include everyone in the classroom or in the programme cohort ... we believe it is better for new academic staff to think holistically about inclusion and not just about dealing with one particular group of students or with any deficit model of student need.
>
> (Grace and Gravestock 2009: 1)

> It is ... important that the curriculum that we develop, the language and visual aids that we use, the materials that we distribute and the methods we use to engage students should be appropriate for a wide range of student identities.
>
> (Grace and Gravestock 2009: 7)

Valli and colleagues endorse this view:

> Inclusive practice is, by definition, not about special treatment of people who are 'other' than 'us', instead it is a set of practices designed to mitigate disadvantage and discrimination. These practices need to be educationally sound for all students, not just the students who are perceived as being from 'different' backgrounds. Inclusive practice is good practice for all.
>
> (Valli et al. 2009: 6)

However, many lecturers welcome specific guidance on key factors to attend to if they are likely to be teaching learners with a particular disability.

The following are examples of what to bear in mind when teaching learners with vision impairments:

1. Where possible, ask a learner how you can best meet their needs and keep checking if they are being met.
2. Consider the physical layout of the room. Ideally it would remain unchanged for the duration of a course or module.
3. Describe and explain images and other visual information clearly.
4. Make copies of material available in advance, along with information such as reading lists and handouts.
5. Provide alternative formats for the material (e.g. electronic) as appropriate.
6. Explore the possibility of recording the session.

The following are examples of things to bear in mind when teaching learners with hearing difficulties:

1. If possible, discuss the learner's requirements in advance and make sure to keep checking that they are being met.
2. It may be easier for the learner to follow the session if they have outline notes that signpost the structure of the information/talk.
3. Check if it would be useful for this to be made available before the session.
4. Be sure to face the learner when you are talking to enable them to lip-read.
5. Be careful not to stand with your back to the window, as this can make you into a silhouette.
6. Remember to repeat any question or comment from the group.
7. If the learner has a support worker, remember to address the learner, not the worker.
8. Occasionally, you may need to pause for the support worker to catch up.

Some elements of good practice become especially important when working with learners with dyslexia. They are included below with other factors to bear in mind.

1. Lay great stress on the structure of any talk or lecture, including dealing with new terminology and key points at the start of the session.
2. Provide a clear framework.
3. Make intermittent summaries connected to the framework.
4. Provide information in small chunks.
5. Make a books list and any other key reading material available in advance of the session.
6. Make clear distinctions between important and background reading.
7. Make sure you provide concrete examples of any abstract ideas.
8. Make full use of material such as video clips, diagrams, and so on, that do not depend on reading text.
9. Be concise, speak directly to the class, and avoid ambiguous language.
10. Minimize the amount of information to be transcribed during a session.
11. Be wary of providing previously unseen material for reading in class.

The above lists are by no means intended to be comprehensive. A wealth of guidance about inclusive teaching is available online. The following are some useful websites:

The Higher Education Academy:
http://www.heacademy.ac.uk/ourwork/teachingandlearning/inclusion/disability

Action on Access – resources linked to Widening Participation:
http://www.actiononaccess.org

SKILL – guides aimed at specific categories of higher education staff, with further links:
http://www.skill.org.uk/page.aspx?c=114&p=204

Open University – inclusive teaching best practice guidance:
http://www.open.ac.uk/inclusiveteaching/pages/inclusive-teaching/index.php

Demos – online materials for staff disability awareness:
http://jarmin.com/demos/

Techdis:
http://www.techdis.ac.uk/resources/files/curricula.pdf

Teachability guidance on accessible teaching:
http://www.teachability.strath.ac.uk/

Strategies for creating inclusive programmes of study:
http://www.scips.worc.ac.uk/

For information on the legal framework and Codes of Practice, go to:

http://www.equalityhumanrights.com/Documents/Disability/Education/
Post16_Code.doc

http://www.equalityhumanrights.com/en/publicationsandresources/Pages/
Understanding theDDA.aspx

QAA
http://www.qaa.ac.uk/academicinfrastructure/codeOfPractice/section3/
default.asp

If you are teaching in a higher education institution, there should be guidance available on making teaching inclusive from a unit or staff involved with learner support.

Question 52: How do you deal with different intelligences in a group?

This question relates to Howard Gardner's concept of multiple intelligences. In his book *Frames of Mind* (1984), Gardner suggested that all of us possess seven intelligences, each developed to a greater or lesser extent:

- *Linguistic intelligence* involves sensitivity to spoken and written language, the ability to learn languages, and the capacity to use language to accomplish certain goals.
- *Logical-mathematical intelligence* involves the capacity to analyse problems logically, carry out mathematical operations, and investigate issues scientifically.
- *Musical intelligence* entails skill in the performance, composition, and appreciation of musical patterns.
- *Spatial intelligence* features the potential to recognize and manipulate the patterns of wide space (those used, for instance, by navigators and pilots) as well as the patterns of more confined areas (such as those of importance to sculptors, surgeons, chess players, graphic artists, and architects).

- *Bodily-kinaesthetic intelligence* entails the potential of using one's whole body or parts of the body (like the hand or the mouth) to solve problems or fashion products.
- *Interpersonal intelligence* denotes a person's capacity to understand the intentions, motivations, and desires of other people and, consequently, to work effectively with others.
- *Intrapersonal intelligence* involves the capacity to understand oneself, to have an effective working model of oneself – including one's own desires, fears, and capacities – and to use such information effectively in regulating one's own life.

(Gardner 1999: 41–43)

Gardner's criteria for identifying an intelligence were drawn from the disciplines of biological sciences, logical analysis, developmental psychology, and traditional psychological research.

In 1999, in *Intelligence Reframed*, Gardner considered the suggestions that had been made for additions to the seven intelligences and, after rejecting a spiritual intelligence and being equivocal about an existential intelligence, opted to add naturalist intelligence to the seven. *Naturalist intelligence* is seen in people expert in recognizing and classifying the varieties of plants and animals in their environment.

The idea of multiple intelligences has been taken up by some involved in the schooling of young children and there are instances of children identifying themselves as 'people smart' or 'number smart', and so on. The case for it in this context is that a child can identify at least one intelligence or talent that they do have and emphasizing this can assist their confidence. It also encourages teachers and children alike to expand their definitions of what intelligence is and invites everyone to ask not 'How intelligent are you?' but 'How are you intelligent?'

If the concept is valid, it could have implications in higher education as well. If being developed in a particular intelligence indicates your preferred way of learning, perhaps the teacher should teach to accommodate the differing intelligence profiles of a group of learners.

The following are learning activities that might be preferred by a person with that particular intelligence:

- *Linguistic*: a variety of text and auditory stimuli; the chance to talk through new concepts; public speaking; creative writing; verbal debate.
- *Logical-mathematical*: using abstract symbols to represent concrete objects and concepts; looking for patterns in ideas and relationships; solving logical puzzles and working out sequences; cause-and-effect analysis; calculating; estimating.
- *Musical*: using rhymes, songs or other rhythmical patterns to aid memory.

- *Spatial*: imagining; drawing; designing; constructing; painting; mind-mapping.
- *Bodily-kinaesthetic*: movement, touch or other physical experiences; hands-on projects; role play; working with objects.
- *Interpersonal*: cooperative learning; considering issues from a range of perspectives; interpersonal problem-solving; giving feedback; receiving feedback; active listening.
- *Intrapersonal*: time for reflection; self-assessment; feelings responses; developing self-awareness.

Task 13

Think of a learning activity you currently use with your learners that appeals to just one or perhaps two of the multiple intelligences. Plan for how you could redesign the activity so that it still achieves the learning objectives but engages more, or different, intelligences in your learners.

The validity of multiple intelligences has been questioned, most notably by John White. He suggests that the foundation upon which Gardner's theory is based does not hold up to scrutiny and that the intelligences have not been proven to exist. But he concludes his critique by asking, is it a bad thing if the use of this theory helps a learner in seeing themselves as possessing one or more intelligences and so 'improves their view of themselves and helps them enjoy their learning? Or, is the idea that we are all different in our innately given abilities in this way just as limiting to our self-perception as IQ theory?' (White 2004: 17).

There are some obvious parallels between the reception given to, and the uses made of, the concept of multiple intelligences and that of learning styles identified by Peter Honey and Alan Mumford. Honey and Mumford adapted Kolb's Learning Styles Inventory and they suggested there are four learning styles – activist, reflector, theorist, and pragmatist – that approximate to the four points on what is commonly referred to as Kolb's learning cycle (see Question 5). A learning style questionnaire is available to help establish your preferred learning style (Honey and Mumford 2000). Honey and Mumford's learning styles were one of thirteen learning style models critically reviewed by Coffield et al. (2004). An outline of the research can be found in Hall and Moseley (2005).

Although the ideas of multiple intelligences and learning styles originate in very different contexts, they both stress that individuals may differ in the way they learn and that these differences can be identified. The response to both ideas and the uses to which they are put are very similar:

- They have been welcomed by some teachers.
- The validity of the concepts has been strongly challenged.
- To recognize that there are differing intelligences or learning styles can be liberating for some learners and it can serve to remind teachers that the chances are that not all members of their class will learn in the way that they did.
- They run the risk of labelling individuals and not encouraging them to develop a repertoire of strengths in intelligence or learning style. As Hall and Moseley note:

> This is the important difference between the use and abuse of learning styles: self-knowledge is not the end point of the process. It is not enough to know oneself to be an 'activist' unless that information helps one to tackle a problem in thinking and learning. We would argue, in fact, that the process of finding oneself to be an 'activist' should include strategies for not being an activist when appropriate … The outcome of engaging with style should be strategy.
>
> (Hall and Moseley 2005: 254)

If you decide to let the concept of multiple intelligences or learning styles inform your teaching, it still leaves the question of how to take account of these. Do you want to accommodate the differences in learners and plan a session that contains something for the activists, the reflectors, the pragmatists, and the theorists or for all intelligences? Or do you want to alert your learners to their preferences and give them the vocabulary to talk about themselves as learners but then help them to develop strategies, as Hall and Moseley suggest, for not becoming too dependent on one type of learning?

Question 53: Can we discuss ways of effectively involving international students in lectures/seminars/tutorials in higher education?

A linked question was:

> 'In terms of cultural differences, how can I get some of my more reluctant discussion participators to talk in class? Some cultures promote a more passive style of learning than here in the UK'.

Difficulties experienced by international students and their tutors are most likely to relate to differing expectations and cultural norms and the resulting lack of understanding of each other's perspective. Language may be a significant factor too, although, as Monika Foster writes, 'it is worth noting that although effective English language skills are an important factor in Chinese students' successful study (as for all international students), ... it is only one of the challenges, and often not the most difficult one to overcome' (Foster 2008: 7).

Janette Ryan notes that 'the "gap" in expectations between lecturers and international students is often the source of students' problems rather than a lack in students' own skills' (Ryan 2005: 93). Citing her earlier research, which involved interviewing lecturers and international students, she identifies the gap as being between on the one hand what students expected and what lecturers thought were 'good' learning and teaching practices, and on the other what the students experienced. Many lecturers had misconceptions that included seeing international students as:

- a homogeneous group with similar learning styles and expectations;
- rote learners with a surface approach to learning;
- unwilling to participate in class discussion;
- only wanting to interact with others from similar backgrounds.

International students reported:

- feeling undervalued and misunderstood;
- wanting to learn new skills, to demonstrate their experience and expertise, speak up and participate but needing help to do so;
- they liked doing group work and using independent and critical approaches to learning.

(Ryan 2005: 93)

Jude Carroll notes that learners who study abroad find that behaviours and assumptions related to learning that have stood them in good stead in their home country may not apply. Teachers become aware of these behaviours and assumptions and may conscientiously attempt to understand the culture that the student comes from. However, she suggests what may be a more effective and practical response for teachers of international students: 'Teachers can help students best by becoming more knowledgeable about their own academic culture' (Carroll 2005: 27). Once teachers can come to see their own culture objectively, they will be in a better position to explain it to international students.

Carroll suggests we should be explicit with our students, which in turn necessitates being self-aware of our own culture, which we may have taken for granted. She notes that lecturers often shy away from giving information to students about academic culture. There are three common reasons:

1. They are 'concerned about appearing patronising or of seeming to criticise students' previous experiences'.

2. They 'believe learning to fit in is part of a student's task'.
3. Or, it is simply too much effort as a result of schedules, workloads or even personal inclination.

(Carroll 2005: 30)

When we are exposed to instances of other cultures, too often we can react with disappointment, seeing international students' behaviour as the negative expression of our own cultural values. Indeed, often it is not until we experience alternatives that we become aware that we have assumptions.

Jude Carroll points to three stages in the process of becoming self-aware of your own academic culture:

1. Identify a behaviour of international students that you find different.
2. Ask what is your assumption that results in you perceiving this as different.
3. Therefore, what is the rule that you are unconsciously applying?

She provides an example: the giving of presents to a teacher by an international student. Presents may be viewed as bribery and 'The British or Australian teacher probably automatically assumes the behaviour has the same (unwelcome) meaning in an international student as it would have in a home student who acted that way' (Carroll 2005: 29). A group of British teachers were asked to identify academic cultural 'rules' that lay behind their reaction to unexpected behaviour by international students and for presents they came up with 'presents are OK but only after the mark has been assigned. The present should be small and preferably disposable/edible. It is more common to send a thank you card or a note' (ibid.: 29). This is one example of articulating to yourself the kind of rules you are adhering to, which can lead you to be surprised at the behaviour of students used to a different set of rules.

Task 14

Here are some examples of behaviours by international students that British lecturers experienced as unexpected:

- Calling me Dr. X even when I have said, call me John.
- Coming into my office after I have given the marks to argue loudly that I should give them higher marks – several times.
- Handing in 4000 words for an essay with a 2500 limit.
- Remaining silent in seminars even when I ask a direct question.

(Carroll 2005: 29)

If you find these 'other', ask in each case what is the assumption and rule that you are operating with?

Once you know what you need to be explicit about – for instance, teacher and student roles or assessment practices or academic writing – then it is your judgement about when to be explicit and how much detail to go into. In teaching a group comprised exclusively of students from Hong Kong, I realized that there may have been some differences in expectations between us relating to the respective roles of teacher and students. When I was in that situation again, I began the module by giving the students a copy of the list below, 'As a student I expect', and asked them to indicate which items from the list matched their expectations. I then found out through a show of hands what the expectations of the class were. I was able to acknowledge this and then be explicit about my expectations and as a group we explored where our expectations differed.

As a student, I expect:

- to be told what to do;
- that the teacher knows more than me;
- to be asked what I want;
- to influence the progress of the session/course;
- to be told if I'm right or wrong;
- to be made welcome;
- to decide for myself what I want to get out of the session/course;
- that the teacher knows what will be covered in a session/course;
- to be helped by other students;
- that I will be encouraged to apply the learning to my personal circumstances;
- that the knowledge I gain will be from the teacher;
- to help other students learn;
- to provide information useful to the teacher;
- that I will make notes;
- to be asked what I think;
- to be asked to evaluate the session/course;
- to ensure that I learn something;
- the teacher to ensure that I learn something.

In the same vein I used a further list, 'As a teacher I expect', to discuss any differences in how I and the students viewed my role.

As a teacher, I expect:

- to make a session plan;
- to assess students;
- to respond to individual needs of students;
- to determine the aims of the session;

- students to assess themselves;
- to allow the students to determine the content and the method;
- to be the principal resource for the students' learning;
- to be solely responsible for the learning that takes place;
- to ensure the group works as a group;
- to allow students to explore and digress;
- to be seen as a manager of learning opportunities.

(Mortiboys 2005: 58–59)

In summary, when working with international students, 'teachers may need to be patient, sensitive and adaptable themselves as well as explicit with students attempting to adjust to Western academic culture' (Carroll 2005: 34).

This strategy of becoming aware of your culture and then being explicit about it can be adapted to assist in answering two other questions, from lecturers new to teaching in higher education in the UK:

> 'What stereotypes am I bringing into the classroom being from another culture?'

> 'I will teach in a different country, culture, and language. What expectation will my students have of a university lecturer?'

Apart from differing expectations and cultural norms, the other area most likely to cause difficulties for international students is language. Ryan notes that the 'areas that international students find most problematic relate to lectures (i.e. understanding lecture content) and to tutorials and seminars (i.e. being able to participate)' (Ryan 2005: 96). Many of these difficulties relate to language and it is important to recognize that ' "Academic" English can be quite different from the "social" English that many students have already mastered' (Valli et al. 2009: 13).

So, when giving a talk or lecture for international students,

- avoid or minimize the use of slang, colloquialisms, acronyms, abbreviations, jargon, idioms or irony;
- take care not to speak too fast;
- articulate clearly;
- use short sentences with simple structures;
- avoid references that depend on cultural knowledge that students may not possess.

Other elements of good practice become even more important when transmitting a great deal of information. These include:

- providing a framework for each lecture, stating its main objectives, and how it links to previous and future topics;
- summarizing the main points of the lecture;
- 'flagging' important information through the use of phrases such as, 'this is a key point';
- pausing after key information or repeating or re-phrasing the information to allow more time for note-taking;
- providing lecture notes in advance or via the web.

(Ryan 2005: 97)

When it comes to participation in group work and seminars, the opportunity to be active and interactive ought to be useful for all learners, as it can help them to check and consolidate their understanding. However, problems with language or lack of knowledge of conventions for participation might prevent that. Ryan cautions:

> If tutors do not respond to the contributions made by international students, because they are difficult to understand or are unfamiliar, the tutor's body language or facial expression can sometimes betray a lack of understanding or acceptance … it takes much courage [for international students] to make a verbal contribution when they know that their language is clumsy and that they may not have understood.
>
> (Ryan 2005: 98)

Good practice such as the formulation and adherence to ground rules in discussion is important if international students are not to be excluded.

This was a strategy of one lecturer I met. If a student whose first language was not English wanted to provide an answer to a question in a session, the lecturer asked them to give the answer to everyone first in their own language, then to say it again in translation. His thinking was that the student needed the opportunity to use their own language to articulate their thoughts. This strategy avoided the problem of simultaneously thinking through an answer and translating it. He reports that it developed confidence and engagement.

Consider three further pointers when working with international students.

1. Be wary of 'stereotyping learners according to the culture or community to which they belong' (Valli et al. 2009: 2). Avoid asking the individual student to speak on behalf of a culture that you perceive them to belong to if only because not every individual will reflect the norms and behaviours of a community.
2. Investigate whether your course materials can be more international, such as using case studies, examples or sources from elsewhere. At the

same time, look to see if you can draw on any different perspectives or experiences that international students might bring with them or ask students to explore how the theory you present might be used differently in their culture.

3. Be directive if necessary in getting international students to work and mix with home students.

9 Evaluation

Question 54: How can I effectively evaluate a session in order to improve the next?

If you want to evaluate a teaching session so as to develop as a teacher, consider your answers to these six questions, which will determine how you go about the evaluation.

From what source will you acquire information on which to base your evaluation?
The most obvious source of information is your learners. Another source is an observer, perhaps a colleague or someone from your university's academic practice and learning and teaching unit. Finally, you can choose to use yourself as a source of information, possibly assisted by an audio or video recording of your performance made of course with the permission of the learners if they are included in it.

Why are you gathering the information and who are you doing it for?
Are you gathering the information to improve or to impress or both? In other words, are you looking to develop in your teaching, as the questioner above? Or, do you want to obtain information for those to whom you are accountable, to use to promote the course or to use as evidence for a teaching portfolio or job application?

Do you want information on every aspect of the session, or just selected aspects?
The observation menu (p. 129 below) lists aspects of your teaching session and so you might choose to gather information about all or some of these. You may want to know about the totality of the learners' experience and so go beyond what happens in contact time and seek information about online resources, accessing other resources, tutorial support, assessment arrangements, and so on.

When are you going to gather the information?
Normally, information from learners will be gathered at the end of or following a session or module. Don't forget that you can also seek information mid-module or at intervals during the module.

How are you going to gather the information?
If asking learners during or at the end of a session, your choice is likely to be written or verbal. The technology available may afford some other alternatives, such as keypads (see Question 21) or uploading comments to a virtual learning environment.

How are you going to deal with the information?
A first thing to be aware of is any tendency you may have to filter the information. Many lecturers become defensive in response to actual or implied criticism and only give credence to the 'good news' or, conversely, the fact that 39/40 responses are positive is ignored as they obsess over the one negative comment. Recognize that your initial reaction to the information gathered may be to be overwhelmed by these emotional responses. Dialogue is the best way to learn from information, so if you can create the opportunity to talk over the feedback with a colleague that can be very productive. If it is feasible to talk over the feedback with the learners, even better.

If you are seeing the group again, tell them what their feedback said – you may even be able to make collated copies of the feedback available in print or online so that all learners can see each others' response. This can be a way of exposing some learners to alternative reactions to the sessions. Tell the learners what their criticisms were and respond to them, changing your practice if you think that is appropriate.

What follows is more detail about using the three sources of information: yourself, your learners, and peer observation.

Using yourself as a source of information

Here are three ways you can do this:

1. *Keeping a diary or log of your experiences*

You may choose to focus on 'critical incidents' – that is, those episodes that are surprising, worrying, revelatory or in some way unusual. Often critical incidents will be times when things went wrong but it is also useful to analyse occasions that went particularly well. In critical incident analysis, it is important to make notes as soon after the incident as you can. It helps if you can describe the episode in detail, including as much content as possible. It can be embellished with your feelings and responses. You might then return to your account over a period of time as aspects of the event become clear or emerge as significant.

Stephen Brookfield suggests a set of questions that can be used in looking back over a week of classes. He devised these for use by learners but also commends their use by the teacher who is looking to reflect regularly on their practice.

- At what moment in the class this week did you feel most engaged with what was happening?
- At what moment did you feel most distant?
- What action that anyone (teacher or student) took did you find most affirming or helpful?
- What action that anyone (teacher or student) took in class did you find most puzzling or confusing?
- What about the class this week surprised you most (this could be your own reactions to what went on, something that someone did, or anything else that occurs to you)?

(Brookfield 1995: 115)

Once you have the information, from asking Brookfield's questions or from the critical incident, then use questions such as the following to help you analyse and learn from the experience:

- What were the significant factors?
- What do I feel about that now?
- What have I learnt from this about …?
- What, if anything, am I going to do about this?
- What would I do differently next time?
- Is there any useful theory I can apply here?

2. Audio or video recording

When viewing a recording of your session, it may be useful to stop the recording at certain points and ask

- What was going on then?
- How did you feel at that point?
- Have you felt like that before?
- What were you thinking?
- What else could you have done at that point?

- What stopped you doing that?
- If you had done that, how would it have felt?

(adapted from Gibbs 1988: section 4.3.2)

3. *Incomplete sentences*

Complete these sentences to trigger a review of your session:

- The part of the session that I found most rewarding was ...
- The one part I would like to do differently if I had the chance would be ...
- I was at my most uncertain when ...
- I was most relaxed when ...
- I felt anxious when ...
- I was pleased with ...
- I felt awkward when ...
- One part of what I said that I could have worded differently was ...

You could also use this device to look more broadly at your practice:

- I feel my greatest strength as a teacher is ...
- I enjoy my work most when ...
- The aspect that I am most pleased with recently has been ...
- I feel my greatest area for development lies in ...
- My learners would benefit more from my expertise if ...
- What's been least successful recently has been ...
- My goal in teaching for the near future is ...
- My goal in teaching for the long-term is ...

Using learners as a source of information

If you use feedback forms with your learners, open questions will provide you with the richest information. Consider the following questions:

- What was useful?
- What would have made it more useful?
- What are you looking for from the remaining sessions of the module?
- What was your overall impression of this session?
- What would you have liked more of?
- What would you have liked less of?
- What was the best part?

- What could be improved?
- What would be your advice to someone thinking of taking this module next year?

The other option with forms is some kind of grading or structured questions. You may be familiar with these from your experience as a learner. Some examples of how these forms are structured are:

The materials were:

> *poor   satisfactory   good   excellent*

The lecture was stimulating:

> *strongly agree   agree   disagree   strongly disagree*

The session prepared me for the assessment:

> *not at all   partially   substantially   completely*

A simple device to prompt verbal feedback with a group of up to about forty is the round (see Question 6).

Using peer observation of teaching

Peer observation can be a very potent device for development. The following is a series of steps to take you through one particular model of the peer observation process.

1. Locate a colleague who is willing to observe you teach. You may want to engage in reciprocal observation. You may find it more help to use someone who is unfamiliar with the material you are teaching. This ensures that the focus stays on how you teach, not the content. If you can find someone with a similar level of experience of teaching that would help.

2. Arrange to meet your colleague in advance of the session to be observed. Use this time to prepare for the observation. Things you may wish to discuss and confirm include:

- The date, time, and place of the observation.
- The duration of the observation.
- Details of the class, including context, module, the learners, the session objectives, plan, activities, materials.
- What aspects of the session you would particularly like to discuss. For example, use of materials, learner participation, use of questioning, clarity of instruction and explanations. You might use the

observation menu below as a prompt for determining the focus for the observation.

- How you will introduce your colleague to the learners.
- How your colleague should behave in the session – joining in or not, taking notes or not, where they should sit.
- When and where to have the post-observation discussion.
- What aspects of the observation and the post-observation discussion, if any, will be recorded and how.
- Confidentiality of what is said and, if appropriate, recorded.
- Contact details.

Observation menu

Setting and using session objectives
Structure of the session
Layout of the room
Learners' responses and behaviour
Suitability of materials
Quality of materials
Use of materials
Use of questions
Explaining skills (perhaps using the full list of these from Question 23)
Use of voice
Enthusiasm
Body language
Attending and listening to the group
Acknowledging individuals
Responding to comments and questions
Readiness to be flexible and responsive
Getting the learners to be active
Being inclusive
Getting feedback about learners' understanding

---

3. Carry out the observation.

4. Meet immediately after the observation or, if this is not possible, as soon as you can for the post-observation discussion. The purpose of this discussion is for the observer to assist you in reviewing your teaching. It should be led by you. The role of your colleague is primarily to:

- Offer observations – details of what they saw in the session, without interpretation or judgement.

- Assist you in your reflection, by asking questions and making other responses that help you to make sense of and learn from what happened.

5. You might choose to make an action plan based upon the outcomes of the discussion.

In this model, the emphasis is on observation of teaching without any form of judgement or assessment by the observer. This is a very important point to realize, as often when the term 'peer observation' is used, teachers hear it as 'peer assessment'. In the role of observer, it is possible to observe a colleague and help them discuss the session afterwards without you, as observer, making any judgement about their performance. Usually, the teacher craves some feedback and the observer is very keen to give some positive feedback and some tips for improvement. However, the more control the teacher has over each aspect of the process – the focus of the observation, the conclusions reached afterwards, and the action plans – the more effective it will be as a development experience for them. With my colleague Jon Dudley, I wrote an account of our project that experimented with this non-judgemental approach (Dudley and Mortiboys 1999). In this model, the experience of observing can be as useful as the experience of being observed. In other words, it uses the observed teaching session as the basis of professional development for the two individuals involved. The following are comments aired by some participants in the project:

> 'the strength of this model is that it removes assessment – it carries no points'

> 'you learn from being involved in teaching and learning without being a teacher or learner' [when in the observer role]

> 'it is crucial to say and hear things about yourself that you would otherwise not admit to in a normal environment'

> 'you give so much to the students – it's lovely having someone talking about _me_'

This non-judgemental model between genuine peers has been described by David Gosling (2005: 13) as the 'collaborative model', one of three models of peer observation that he identifies. The other one of these three that is designed to help the observed teacher is the 'developmental' model, where staff with expertise advise or facilitate on how to improve teaching. (The primary concern of the third model – 'evaluative' – is to arrive at judgements, determine quality, or monitor progress and may only incidentally be helpful in the development of the teacher.)

If you do want to introduce judgement and make it closer to a peer *assessment* of teaching, you would need to turn items on the observation menu above into something resembling criteria that indicate good or satisfactory practice. For example:

- Learning objectives were clear
- The structure of the session was well balanced
- The room layout was appropriate, and so on.

If you do observe a colleague, consider the different ways of initiating discussion after the session. Here are three ways:

- *Giving a verdict*: 'It would have been better if you had used open questions more'.
- *Drawing the teacher's attention to what was happening*: 'I noticed all of the questions you asked were closed questions'.
- *Inviting the teacher to reflect*: 'What thoughts do you have on your use of questioning?'

Of course, there any many more aspects of your work as a teacher other than what you do in the teaching session. For this reason, peer observation of teaching has been criticized for having too narrow a focus. David Gosling and Kristine Mason O'Connor (2009) have suggested that peer-supported review could draw on the same principles of peer observation of teaching but be used to look at other aspects of the teacher's role in supporting learning, such as preparation of materials, creating assessments, marking, creating and using online tools.

10 Excellence

Question 55: What are your top three tips for being an excellent teacher?

This is probably the hardest question of all and responding to it is tempting but probably ill-advised.

What makes an 'excellent teacher' depends of course on what you mean by 'teacher' and what you mean by 'excellent'. The differing interpretations of what it means to teach have been touched on briefly in Question 13. The question of what excellence in teaching in higher education looks like has attracted a great deal of interest in higher education institutions in recent times, leading to the development of many teaching excellence awards. One thing that is clear is that there is no consensus on what excellence is. Graham Gibbs (2007) illustrated this strikingly in his article *Have we lost the plot with teaching awards?* He investigated a wide range of teaching excellence schemes in the UK and mainland Europe and found twelve different conceptions of teaching excellence:

1. No conception.
2. Excellent teaching is characterized by observable teacher behaviours, primarily in the classroom.
3. Excellent teaching is characterized by the quality of its attention to student learning.
4. Excellent teaching is characterized by engagement in the 'scholarship of teaching'.

   (a) Undertaking reflection.
   (b) Being able to articulate a personal philosophy of teaching.
   (c) Making use of pedagogic literature.
   (d) Undertaking pedagogic research.

5. Excellent teaching is characterized by the benefits derived from the teacher's research.

   (a) Undertaking 'research-based' teaching.
   (b) Basing teaching on the teacher's own 'scholarship of integration'.
   (c) Displaying 'pedagogic subject knowledge'.

6. Excellent teaching involves a focus on the personal and intellectual development of the individual student.

   (a) Nurturing the development of individuals.
   (b) Inducting students into the (disciplinary or professional) community.

7. Excellent teaching is characterized by a focus on students' overall experience of their course or entire programme.

   (a) Creating effective courses or programmes.
   (b) Collaborating in teaching teams.

8. Excellent teachers display 'good citizenship'.
9. Excellent teaching involves innovation and change.
10. Excellent teachers develop the teaching of others.
11. Excellence in teaching is defined by the institution's Corporate Plan.
12. Excellent teaching is whatever colleagues recognize as excellent.

(Gibbs 2007: 40–42)

In informal discussions, staff and students at Roehampton University identified twenty-three dimensions of teaching excellence (Burden et al. 2006). For students, the three most important dimensions were:

- range of strategies/techniques
- enthusiasm/inspiration
- teaching for 'learning that lasts'

For staff, the three most important dimensions were:

- enthusiasm/inspiration
- subject-specific knowledge
- communication/interpersonal skills

Sally Brown (2003) drafted *Differentiating good and excellent teaching: is it possible?* with suggestions and amendments from sixteen people working in educational development in higher education. She suggested that exemplary teachers:

- Ensure that all aspects of the learning programme are 'constructively aligned' so that the programme is truly reflected in its delivery mechanisms, assessment, and evaluation.
- Engage in critical thinking about learning and teaching, influence others by their own purposiveness, and can communicate why their practice is successful.
- Inspire and motivate students to learn effectively, not just capable and autonomous learners, but also those who struggle to understand and apply knowledge. Make complex ideas accessible.
- Demonstrate passion and enthusiasm for their subject, for learning, and for learners. Seek out good practice that is transferable from other contexts. Take leading roles in their subject communities.
- Are recognized by their peers and their own learning and teaching community as activists who are engaged in the advancement of understanding about pedagogic issues.
- Constructively engage with the diverse student body to enhance the learning of the group as a whole. Bring specialist knowledge of one or more aspects of diversity to their own practice and share this with other practitioners.
- Have an outstanding track record in disseminating good practice and sharing efficiency.
- Analyse, sustain, and advance those innovations across their own institutions, subject groupings, and beyond.
- Are regarded by students as highly supportive, empathetic, and as positive role models. Able to challenge and disrupt fixed ideas/ complacency.
- Actively work to ensure that the resources and opportunities provided by their institution are captured and effectively utilized, work to improve the learning and teaching context locally and nationally, challenge inappropriate or irrelevant practice, engage actively and imaginatively with the mission of the institution.
- Are identified by students as 'going the extra mile' in terms of their commitment to help their students succeed.
- Actively seek feedback and critical appraisal from peers and provide supportive feedback to colleagues within and beyond their subject areas.
- Support students in recognizing their learning styles and developing new strategies for deep learning and transforming students' ways of thinking.

What this suggests is that excellent teaching goes beyond being directly responsible for quality learning of your learners and includes, among other things, promoting and sharing good practice and innovation.

David Kember with Carmel McNaught interviewed 62 academics nominated by their universities as being exemplary or noteworthy teachers and from these interviews derived the following 'principles of good teaching':

1. Teaching and curriculum design needs to be consistent with meeting students' future needs. This implies the development of a range of generic capabilities, including:

   - self-managed learning ability;
   - critical thinking;
   - analytical skills;
   - teamwork;
   - leadership;
   - communication skills.

2. Ensure that students have a thorough understanding of fundamental concepts, if necessary at the expense of covering excessive content.

3. Establish the relevance of what is taught by:

   - using real-life examples;
   - drawing cases from current issues;
   - giving local examples;
   - relating theory to practice.

4. Challenging beliefs is important to:

   - establish appropriate ways of learning and beliefs about knowledge;
   - deal with misconceptions of fundamental concepts.

5. Meaningful learning is most likely to occur when students are actively engaged with a variety of learning tasks. Discussion is an important learning activity.

6. Establishing empathetic relationships with students is a prerequisite to successful interaction with them. To do this you need to know them as individuals.

7. Good teachers accept that it is their responsibility to motivate students to achieve the high expectations they have of them. Motivation comes through:

- encouraging students;
- the enthusiasm of the teacher;
- interesting and enjoyable classes;
- relevant material;
- a variety of active learning approaches.

8. Planning programmes and courses involves consideration of students' future needs. The plans ensure that aims, fundamental concepts, learning activities, and assessment are consistent with achieving outcomes related to future student needs. Feedback needs to be gathered to inform each of these elements in the curriculum design process.
9. Thorough planning is needed for each lesson, but plans need to be adapted flexibly in light of feedback obtained in class.
10. Assessment must be consistent with the desired learning outcomes and eventual student needs if these are to be achieved. Assessment should, therefore, be authentic tasks for the discipline or profession.

(Kember and McNaught 2007: viii–ix)

From the above accounts, it is evident that being an 'excellent teacher' means more than being effective in the lecture theatre or classroom. However, this book has focused on questions that are most pressing for new lecturers. These are mostly about teaching groups of learners face-to-face, although some of the answers have hopefully conveyed that what happens in contact time is inextricably bound up with other factors in the learner experience outside of the 'session', not least curriculum design and especially assessment.

So, I hope that makes it clear why offering 'three top tips' is perhaps unwise. However, it is tempting to try, just to see if the three can be alliterative, in which case you could say that excellent teaching is about being:

- prepared, positive, and persevering, or
- enthusiastic, empowering and empathic, or even
- responsive, resilient and resourceful.

In fact, David Halpin (2003, 2007), in arguing for the importance of Utopianism and Romanticism in education, does suggest there are three essentials for success as a teacher:

- hope, optimism, and perseverance.

On a more mundane level, you could say that in the face-to-face encounter with learners, there are just two sets of skills, knowledge, and qualities that you need, one for an effective presentation, one for ensuring participation.

Skills required for an effective presentation	Skills required to ensure participation
Organizing appropriate content	Organizing appropriate activities
Clarity in delivery	Clarity in giving instructions
Knowledge of subject	Knowledge of how people learn (and knowledge of subject)
Materials to show the learners	Materials for learners to use
Variety in visuals	Variety in activities
Explaining skills	Listening skills
Confidence in talking to people	Confidence in talking with people
Preparation	Preparation
Timekeeping	Timekeeping
Enthusiasm!	Enthusiasm!

I think I am going to go for just one 'tip', one golden rule:

> *Get as far as you can into the perspective of your learners and tailor your planning, your approach, and your response to the group accordingly.*

In essence, be as 'student-centred' as you are 'subject-centred' in planning and delivering your sessions. The term 'student-centred' suffers from a variety of interpretations but in this sense has great value. It means you need to devote sufficient energy to finding out or speculating on the answers to these questions about your group before and during the session:

- How much do they already know?
- What do they want to learn?
- What do they need to learn?
- Why are they here?
- How do they feel about being here? Will they be welcoming or resistant?
- What might their previous relevant experiences have been?
- What are their expectations?
- How are they responding during the session?

After all, this book derives from this approach, of asking learners to write down:

> 'the one question you would like an answer to before the end of the course'.

References

Anderson, L.W. and Krathwohl, D.R. (eds.) (2001) *A Taxonomy for Learning, Teaching, and Assessing: A Revision of Bloom's Taxonomy of Educational Objectives*. New York: Longman.

Angelo, T. (2003) *Finding out how well they're learning what we're teaching: techniques and guidelines for effective classroom feedback*. Keynote address, The UK's Institute for Learning and Teaching in Higher Education (ILTHE) Annual Conference, Warwick, 3 July.

Angelo, T.A. and Cross, K.P. (1993) *Classroom Assessment Techniques: A Handbook for College Teachers* (2nd edn.) San Francisco, CA: Jossey-Bass.

Berk, R.A. (2003) *Professors are from Mars, Students are from Snickers: How to Write and Deliver Humor in the Classroom and in Professional Presentations*. Sterling, VA: Stylus.

Biggs, J. (1987) *Student Approaches to Learning and Studying*. Hawthorn, VIC: Australian Council for Educational Research.

Biggs, J. (2003) *Teaching for Quality Learning at University* (2nd edn.). Buckingham: Open University Press/Society for Research into Higher Education.

Biggs, J. and Tang, C. (2007) *Teaching for Quality Learning at University* (3rd edn.). Maidenhead: Open University Press/Society for Research into Higher Education.

Bligh, D. (1998) *What's the Use of Lectures?* (5th edn.). Exeter: Intellect Books.

Bloom, B.S. (1956) *Taxonomy of Educational Objectives*. New York: David Mackay.

Boniwell, I. (2008) *Positive Psychology in a Nutshell*. London: PWBC.

Boud, D. (2001) Introduction: making the move to peer learning, in D. Boud, R. Cohen and J. Sampson (eds.) *Peer Learning in Higher Education*. London: Kogan Page.

Brookfield, S.D. (1995) *Becoming a Critically Reflective Teacher*. San Francisco, CA: Jossey-Bass.

Brown, S. (2003) Differentiating good and excellent teaching: is it possible?, *Exchange*, 5: 32.

Buckingham, M. and Clifton, D.O. (2005) *Now Discover Your Strengths*. London: Pocket Books.

Burden, P., Bond, C. and Hall, J. (2006) Defining excellence in learning and teaching, *Educational Developments*, 7 (2): 8–10.

Carroll, J. (2005) Strategies for becoming more explicit, in J. Carroll and J. Ryan (eds.) *Teaching International Students*. Abingdon: Routledge.

Claxton, G. (1998) *Hare Brain, Tortoise Mind*. London: Fourth Estate.

Coffield, F., Moseley, D., Hall, E. and Ecclestone, K. (2004) *Learning Styles and Pedagogy in Post-16 Learning: A Systematic and Critical Review*. London: Learning Skills Research Centre.

Csikszentmihalyi, M. (1997) *Finding Flow: The Psychology of Engagement with Everyday Life*. New York: Basic Books.

Davies, P. (2003) *Practical Ideas for Enhancing Lectures*. SEDA Special #13. London: Staff and Educational Development Association.

Dudley, J. and Mortiboys, A. (1999) *Implications of using peer observation to improve the quality of teaching in higher education*, in Proceedings of International Conference on Teacher Education, Hong Kong.

Elton, L. (1996) Strategies to enhance student motivation: a conceptual analysis, *Studies in Higher Education*, 21 (1): 57–68.

Entwistle, N. and Ramsden, P. (1983) *Understanding Student Learning*. London: Croom Helm.

Exley, K. and Dennick, R. (2004) *Small Group Teaching: Tutorials, Seminars and Beyond*. London: RoutledgeFalmer.

Exley, K. and Dennick, R. (2009) *Giving a Lecture: From Presenting to Teaching*. Abingdon: Routledge.

Fineburg, A.C. (2004) Introducing positive psychology to the introductory psychology student, in P.A. Linley and S. Joseph (eds.) *Positive Psychology in Practice*. Hoboken, NJ: Wiley.

Flocker, M. (2006) *Death by PowerPoint: A Modern Office Survival Guide*. Cambridge, MA: Da Capo Press.

Foster, M. (2008) *Enhancing the Experience of Chinese Students in UK Higher Education: Lessons from a Collaborative Project*. SEDA Special #23. London: Staff and Educational Development Association.

Gardner, H. (1984) *Frames of Mind: The Theory of Multiple Intelligences*. London: Heinemann.

Gardner, H. (1999) *Intelligence Reframed: Multiple Intelligences for the 21st Century*. New York: Basic Books.

Gibbs, G. (1981) *Twenty Terrible Reasons for Lecturing*. Occasional Paper #8. Birmingham: SCED.

Gibbs, G. (1988) *Learning by Doing: A Guide to Teaching and Learning Methods*. Oxford: Further Education Unit, Oxford Polytechnic.

Gibbs, G. (2007) Have we lost the plot with teaching awards?, *Exchange*, 7: 40–42.

Gosling, D. (2005) *Peer Observation of Teaching*. SEDA Paper #118. London: Staff and Educational Development Association.

Gosling, D. and Mason O'Connor, K. (eds.) (2009) *Beyond Peer Observation of Teaching*. London: Staff and Educational Development Association.

Grace, S. and Gravestock, P. (2009) *Inclusion and Diversity*. Abingdon: Routledge.

Hall, E. and Moseley, D. (2005) Is there a role for learning styles in personalised education and training?, *International Journal of Lifelong Education*, 24 (3): 243–255.

Halpin, D. (2003) *Hope and Education: The Role of the Utopian Imagination*. London: RoutledgeFalmer.

Halpin, D. (2007) *Romanticism and Education: Love, Heroism and Imagination in Pedagogy*. London: Continuum.

Hattie, J. (2003) *Teachers make a difference: what is the research evidence?*, Paper presented at the Australian Council for Educational Research Annual Conference on Building Teacher Quality, Melbourne, VIC.

Honey, P. and Mumford, A. (2000) *The Learning Styles Questionnaire*. Maidenhead: Peter Honey.

Huston, T. (2009) *Teaching What You Don't Know*. London: Harvard University Press.

Jensen, E. (1995) *The Learning Brain*. San Diego, CA: The Brain Store.

Johnson, L. (1996) *Being an Effective Academic*. Oxford: Oxford Centre for Staff Development.

Keller, J. (2003) Is PowerPoint the Devil?, *Chicago Tribune*, 22 January.

Kember, D. with McNaught, C. (2007) *Enhancing University Teaching: Lessons from Research into Award-winning Teachers*. London: Routledge.

Kolb, D. (1984) *Experiential Learning: Experience as the Source of Learning and Development*. London: Prentice Hall.

Lee, A.Y. and Bowers, A.N. (1997) *The effect of multimedia components on learning*, in Proceedings of the Human Factors and Ergonomics Society 41st Annual Meeting.

Liesveld, R., Miller, J.A. and Robison, J. (2005) *Teach with Your Strengths: How Great Teachers Inspire Their Students*. New York: Gallup Press.

Marton, F. and Saljo, R. (1976a) On qualitative differences in learning – I: outcome and process, *British Journal of Educational Psychology*, 46: 4–11.

Marton, F. and Saljo, R. (1976b) On qualitative differences in learning – II: outcome as a function of the learner's conception of the task, *British Journal of Educational Psychology*, 46: 115–127.

Marton, F., Hounsell, D. and Entwistle, N. (eds.) (1997) *The Experience of Learning*. Edinburgh: Scottish Academic Press.

Mazikunas, G., Panayiotidis, A. and Burke, L. (2009) Changing the nature of lectures using a personal response system, *Innovations in Education and Teaching International*, 46 (2): 199–212.

McCarron, K. and Savin-Baden, M. (2008) Compering and comparing: stand-up comedy and pedagogy, *Innovations in Education and Teaching International*, 45 (4): 355–363.

McGill, I. and Beaty, L. (2001) *Action Learning*. London: Kogan Page.

Mortiboys, A. (2002) *The Emotionally Intelligent Lecturer*. SEDA Special #12. London: Staff and Educational Development Association.

Mortiboys, A. (2005) *Teaching with Emotional Intelligence*. London: Routledge.

Mosteller, F. (1989) The 'muddiest point in the lecture' as a feedback device, *On Teaching and Learning: The Journal of the Harvard-Danforth Centre*, 3: 10–21.

Naughton, J. (2003) PowerPoint panders to our weakest points, *Observer*, 14 January.

Newman-Ford, L.E., Fitzgibbon, K., Lloyd, S. and Thomas, S. (2008) A large-scale investigation into the relationship between attendance and attainment: a study using an innovative, electronic attendance monitoring system, *Studies in Higher Education*, 33 (6): 699–717.

Palmer, P.J. (1997) *The Courage to Teach*. San Francisco, CA: Jossey-Bass.

Parkin, M. (1998) *Tales for Trainers*. London: Kogan Page.

Race, P. (2005) *Making Learning Happen*. London: Sage.

Race, P. (2006) *The Lecturer's Toolkit*. London: Kogan Page.

Race, P. and Pickford, R. (2007) *Making Teaching Work*. London: Sage.

Ramsden, P. (2003) *Learning to Teach in Higher Education*. London: Routledge.

Rust, C. (2001) *A Briefing on Assessment of Large Groups*. York: Learning and Teaching Support Network.

Ryan, J. (2005) Improving teaching and learning practices for international students: implications for curriculum, pedagogy and assessment, in J. Carroll and J. Ryan (eds.) *Teaching International Students*. Abingdon: Routledge.

Schreiner, L.A. and Anderson, E. (2005) Strengths-based advising: a new lens for higher education, *NACADA Journal*, 25 (2): 20–27.

Seligman, M. (2006) *Learned Optimism*. New York: Vintage Books.

Shaw, J. (2001) How to turn thrifty lectures into rich jazz recitals, *Times Higher Educational Supplement*, 21 September.

Toohey, S. (1999) *Designing Courses for Higher Education*. Buckingham: Open University Press.

Tufte, E.R. (2006) *The Cognitive Style of PowerPoint: Pitching Out Corrupts Within* (2nd edn.). Cheshire, CT: Graphics Press.

Valli, Y., Brown, S. and Race, P. (2009) *Cultural Inclusivity: A Guide for Leeds Met Staff*. Leeds: Leeds Metropolitan University.

White, J. (2004) *Howard Gardner: The Myth of Multiple Intelligences*. London: Institute of Education, University of London.

Zull, J.E. (2002) *The Art of Changing the Brain: Enriching the Practice of Teaching by Exploring the Biology of Learning*. Sterling, VA: Stylus.

Index

Related books from Open University Press
Purchase from www.openup.co.uk or order through your local bookseller

---

TEACHING AT COLLEGE AND UNIVERSITY
Effective Strategies and Key Principles
Sarah Moore, Gary Walsh, and Angélica Rísquez

- How can I become an effective teacher in college or university?
- What teaching tools and techniques are available to me and what is the best way to use them?
- How do I tackle common difficulties associated with college and university teaching?

This book is designed for teachers in further and higher education, particularly those who do not have specialist backgrounds in education, pedagogy or academic practice. It presents useful theory and literature from the fields of organizational behaviour, learning, pedagogy and education, to enhance the practical advice the book contains.

A range of evidence-based insights are examined in order to help support the delivery of academic expertise both within and beyond classroom settings. The book also encourages teachers to adopt a reflective orientation and to try out different classroom, interactive or discursive activities and tactics that have been successfully used in similar settings.

In addition, this book helps teachers from across the disciplines not only to develop effective skills in conventional classroom settings (lecture halls, tutorial rooms, one-to-one student consultations) but to consider new approaches to online, blended, and distance learning.

Teaching at College and University provides the most practical evidence-based resource for those involved in teaching at universities and colleges, as well as researchers and policy makers with an interest in good practice in academic settings.

Contents
Developing your self-awareness as a teacher – Focusing on key teaching skills and competencies – Focusing on your students – Exploring and using teaching technologies – Interacting with the institution: managing time, tasks and expectations – Assessment and evaluation – Minding yourself: Focusing on health and well-being – Conclusion – Bibliography – Index.

2007   168pp   978–0–335–22109–7 (Paperback)

TEACHING FOR QUALITY LEARNING AT UNIVERSITY 3e

John Biggs and Catherine Tang

Teaching for Quality Learning at University focuses on implementing a constructively aligned outcomes-based model at both classroom and institutional level. The theory, which is now used worldwide as a framework for good teaching and assessment, is shown to:

- Assist university teachers who wish to improve the quality of their own teaching, their students' learning and their assessment of learning outcomes
- Aid staff developers in providing support for teachers
- Provide a framework for administrators interested in quality assurance and enhancement of teaching across the whole university

The book's "how to" approach addresses several important issues: designing high level outcomes, the learning activities most likely to achieve them in small and large classes, and appropriate assessment and grading procedures. It is an accessible, jargon-free guide to all university teachers interested in enhancing their teaching and their students' learning, and for administrators and teaching developers who are involved in teaching-related decisions on an institution-wide basis. The authors have also included useful web links to further material.

Contents

2007   360pp   978–0–335–22126–4 (Paperback)

THE FIRST YEAR AT UNIVERSITY
Teaching Students in Transition

Bill Johnston

The first year at university can be a very challenging time for students especially in a mass system of higher education. Many students are ill-equipped to cope with life at university and retention is now a critical metric for all universities. This has resulted in universities having to spend considerable time and attention on ensuring that the 'first year experience' is as positive as possible for all students.

This book offers a range of practical strategies, underpinned by relevant research, which lecturers can implement when charged with working with first year students in order to ease their transition to higher education. These strategies affect not only the design of courses, teaching and assessment but also how teams of lecturers provide consistent support, and how this in turn is supported by strategic planning at an institutional level.

The First Year at University is a practical resource that can be used by a wide range of lecturers including those undertaking the PGCE (Higher Education) as well as those on CPD courses on teaching and learning in higher education.

Contents
Preface – Acknowledgements – First year in a mass higher education system – What do we know about teaching first year students, and what should we do with that knowledge? – The first year experience and the academic mainstream – Course design for FYE: a case study – Institutional strategy and the first year experience – Universities in a changing world: grand narratives and modest proposals – Appendix – References – Index.

2010   208pp   978–0–335–23451–6 (Paperback)
                     978–0–335–23450–9 (Hardback)